LIVING LIFE IN THE GREY ZONE

ZONE

A TRUE STORY

LAURA MARIE

First Printing August 2017
ISBN 978-0-9959152-0-6

Printed in The United States of America

Cover photo by Yana Sirenko Used by permission

www.livinglifeinthegreyzone.com

FORWARD

WHEN YOU ARE given the opportunity to become vulnerable, exposed, or transparent, do you embrace it? Run from it? Or even wonder why anyone would want to do so? I have done all those things…depending, of course, on the situation. Laura asked me to write this forward because I was the only person who has seen her transformation over the past eight years. While I know this to be true, it deeply saddened my heart to think that I'm the one person who could say something about her transformation considering I lived 1,500 miles away from seeing it with my own eyes. Honestly, my first thoughts when she asked me were, "I really have nothing to say," and, "I haven't seen you physically in six years."

I humbly tell you that I have lived life with Laura as she's experienced her metamorphosis from an isolated caterpillar who preferred the safety of her cocoon, to the butterfly who lives in the freedom of Christ and who shares his truth, beauty, and goodness that only comes from a gracious, merciful and loving God.

I met Laura at my church in New Orleans where I had been attending for many years. We ate together, prayed together and worshipped together. We shared our lives together as friends and sisters in Christ for a couple of years. Then she left. She moved back to her beloved home country of Canada. I was saddened by the loss of sharing my life with her here—she spoke truth to me about my own weaknesses and even in her own pain unknown to me then, pointed me to the face of a faithful Saviour. We have remained connected virtually and by phone but have not spent face-to-face time with one another since she left.

In those six years since I've seen her as she's suffered many hardships but she has never said "never" to Jesus…even when she wanted to shut the door to him and everyone else forever.

Several years after she moved away, she shared her gut-wrenching story with me. And while it stopped me in my tracks in the moment, it also made my life with Laura make sense. Her shame regarding her lack of truthfulness with me was authentic, and her repentance was real.

For a Jewish girl from California transplanted into Louisiana who became a born-again Christian and after twenty-five years of regularly being asked, "How does a Jew become a Christian?" I've learned about authentically being who I am—a Jewish Christian, just like the first followers of Christ. In looking at my own history regarding my lack of truthfulness, authenticity, and lack of wanting to be known, I grew into a woman who wanted to be truthful, authentic and known. Therefore, forgiveness for Laura was easy to extend. Why may you ask? Because of the forgiveness I have received and continue to receive from my Lord and Saviour, Jesus Christ. Laura wanted to live a life of truth and authenticity and be known for who she is and how she was created by God, defects and all. So, who am I to stop or block her from being her best self for Him?

From the time that Laura revealed her 'Life in the Grey Zone,' I have journeyed with her through her highs and lows, joys and sorrows and the hate and love she has experienced. I have seen her life become real, from her life of extreme bitterness, due to years of neglect, abandonment, and isolation, through her diagnosis of her finally-understood biological birth defect. And further, her personal revelation from John 9 that she was "born this way" so that "God's glory [can] be seen" in and through her - through seasons of acceptance and rejection by Christians. To now live in a community of saints who love, accept and support her in sharing her story, of her manifesting His love through her for others, no matter their circumstances or experiences.

Laura's book is an unforgettable opportunity for you to experience one person's transformation, from a lifetime of being unknown, rejected, alone and retaliatory, to one who has become known, trusting Him and giving to others freely. Now she is keenly aware of her chief purpose for Him; making Him known by the love she has for you.

As her friend and sister in Christ, I encourage you to step away from your own thoughts and beliefs and seek to understand for yourself, even in all of its uncomfortableness, the resounding difference that Jesus Christ has on a life that is lived raw and authentic, for the first time and now, for the rest of her God-given time.

May your experience in reading this book cause, you who are partaker of this same Christ, to run headlong into a fresh experience of His love. For you who do not know Him, I pray you would stop in your tracks to see your need for the deepest love you will ever know.

There is more to life than black and white. Life exists in the grey zone. I pray you are "touched by the grace of Christ" and filled with His love.

Invite her in. You will never be the same.

I love you, my friend.

Tracy

This book is dedicated to the classiest lady I've ever known. You taught me more than you will ever know.

I miss you, Mom.

"The journey to live from grace and not judgment is one Papa takes us on. I've not always been in the place I am today. I've used my Bible knowledge to quote scripture and be smug in my "knowing." It's not until we learn the spirit of mercy and grace for ourselves that we begin to live from the heart of Jesus. He didn't go around quoting scripture to the hurt and broken and outcast. He used scripture on the Pharisees. I'm a recovering Pharisee and so are most Christians."

Susie Scarborough

Acknowledgements

FIRST, I WANT to thank God for everything he has done in my life. You are the reason I'm breathing. I thank you for saving me and giving me your heart. May this book and my life be pleasing to you my Saviour and my friend.

To Tracy McCullough. What can I possibly say to articulate my love for you? You walked with me since 2009. When I was alone and desperate, you were there for me. You have stood by me when all others departed from my life. This book is about love, and you have shown me so much of that. I'm thankful for you. God bless you, dear sister.

To Amie Medeiros. You have struggled to love me and yet, in your gentle and quiet way, you have lavished such love on me, and I wasn't even aware of it. You love on others without fanfare but with a heart that sings his praise, and you do it quietly and with great care. My love for you is inexpressible. I treasure you in my life, and I'm thankful that you stuck with me, and are now seeing me complete and at home with Christ, and that our friendship is now benefiting from the newfound peace and freedom I walk in.

To Njoki and Foster Owusu. What a blessing you both are in my life. I am honoured and delighted to call you not only my brother and sister in Christ but friends as well. Your guidance and godly counsel have been invaluable to me, and I treasure the time that we spend together.

To Angela Tenthory. I don't deserve you as a friend, I truly don't. You are God's love manifested. I am so thankful that you chose to hang in there with me. Your calm, wise words of advice have always been a blessing, and you are such a delight to be near. I am deeply honoured to call you a friend.

To Joe Tenthory. You are truly a gentleman in every sense of the word. I sincerely respect you, and I am so pleased that God has you right where you're needed. Your passion for him, and those you serve is a monument to what God can do with a willing heart. But, above all else, you're just a very kewl guy and a blessing to so many.

There are so many others; Colin and Joy Cook, Wendy and Ken Lawson, Susie Scarborough, Peter and Jean Davidson, Diane Heard and Linda Pease Reed. Thank you all for your love and support. This book would not exist if it weren't for all of you.

SOMETIMES THE best solution we muster up is to give up. The better solution, however, is to let God show you when to give up because so many times his marvellous plan contains victory in an area that has no hope, and all seems lost!

Daily I stand at that crossroads in so many areas of my life as decisions are made. Perhaps the best solution is to wait and trust, and rest beside the still waters, hope in miracles, and faith in the power of the spirit to move mountains, change circumstances, and the hearts and minds of others—most of all mine!

Dear Lord, may I trust you today, and embrace knowing that you have a bigger plan than what I can see. May I hope with absolute childlike abandon and wonder, not at how it will end in misery and despair but how you will change the circumstances, bring hope where there's no hope, and bring glory to you in the process! Let me not dwell on the present mountain before me but help me to see the victory you have prepared for me. Help me embrace these difficult steps of faith I take today, on this narrow path toward that finish line!

Laura Marie

INTRODUCTION

BECAUSE SOMEONE asked me, there was a time that I could share God's love, and the gospel to a group of non-believers. And I did it in a place where it was forbidden to do so, and yet, I shared without repercussions. How was I able to do that? Because when asked, I shared my personal testimony.

No one could 'debate the Bible' with me, or even complain that I was preaching to them because I shared my own personal story, my relationship with Jesus, and how he's changed my life.

In the end, the gospel was spoken, but it wasn't up for debate or complaint because it was lodged within my personal story, my testimony. Who could argue my own story? It was mine, and I shared what God had done for me, as the Bible tells us to be ready to do.

In the same way, this is a book about my life—my story. It's simply my journey, told as best as I can remember it. There will be those who will want to argue it but it's my story, and quite honestly, as with my personal testimony, you have no standing to argue anything.

This book isn't in any way to say that I've arrived in my walk with Christ. Actually, the longer I follow Christ, the more I realize just how blind I truly am (John 9:39), and how desperately I need him.

As Christians, we all face difficult circumstances in our lives. What sets us apart is in how we deal with them as believers. When a non-believer sees us walking in peace and trusting in him, when in the natural, we should be a mess, it can open up a real dialogue with them as to how we can be so calm in the face of disaster or loss, and how our relationship with Jesus makes that all possible.

Not only did Jesus go to great lengths to speak to this point in Scripture, but he also showed us by his own actions that we must be different. We must think differently and live differently. We must seek the real heart of Christ and follow him, walking in his grace, mercy and love; taking on his heart to build bridges, trust, understanding and his genuine love for all those we encounter. To have his heart to see everyone as a gift from God, and not see them as enemies, in particular for those who do us wrong.

This book is about my journey to overcome. It's about my life's struggles, and how in the end he has been beautifully glorified as he's helped me truly come to a place of genuine peace in my life! This is for me, a celebration of life and trust, and ultimately, as the Apostle Paul wrote, 'being content in every circumstance.' (Philippians 4:12-13)

I hesitate even putting my story to paper, despite the MANY Christians begging me to do so over the recent years. But, it was tonight, at a Christmas Day dinner, that God spoke to me through two very close Christian friends. They strongly suggested I put my story to paper, because, as one of them put it, "Your story really affected me. Imagine what it can do for someone in Australia, who will never meet you but because you wrote it down..."

So, here we are.

This is a story about the agonizing pain of a lifetime of isolation. Yet, in the end, it's just a story about God's love, and one that I hope will help you.

I also hope that it helps you deepen your appreciation of the vastness of God's creation in our lives and that you will come to see that the world is far more grey than we ever considered.

I hope this book, through my personal journey, can help you know that there's hope in Christ. For most of my life, I didn't believe there was hope for me at all. I walked a sad, isolated and hopeless existence from before the age of five, to not that many years ago. Yet, today, I know without a doubt there's hope in our Saviour!

But beyond that hope, there's joy! Joy no matter the circumstances. A joy that is unending, and a joy that propels us to forever want to dance and praise him. It's a joy that sent David before the ark to celebrate and proclaim the joy of our Lord, and the joy that helped Paul tell the Philippians so many times in one letter to rejoice!

Joy is the ultimate demonstration of the freedom we have in our Christ-filled hearts.

It's my prayer for you today that you may know this joy first-hand. Dance, and share with others the incredible joy we have in him when God's love is in us, and we love as he loved, and live as he lived.

So, with all that said, come with me as we journey into my life, and discover what the title means—living life in the grey zone.

Part 1

Welcome to the Grey Zone

Chapter 1

"You made all the delicate, inner parts of my body and knit me together in my mother's womb. Thank you for making me so wonderfully complex! Your workmanship is marvellous—how well I know it." Psalm 139:13-14NLT

I WAS BORN the youngest of five children, and for my 40-year-old mother, I would be her last. Her pregnancy with me was normal, and after eight hours of labour, I arrived just after midnight in December of 1964.

Unfortunately, for me, I was born in the grey zone.

What put me in the grey zone was that I was born with a very rare, and virtually unknown, congenital genetic birth defect called 'Partial Androgen Insensitivity Syndrome' PAIS for short. (There's also a much more common version called full AIS.)

How rare is PAIS?

Well, the chances of your child developing Downs syndrome is 1:200 to 1:10 depending on the mother's age. Full AIS is estimated to be

1:2000 to 1:20,000 births. Partial AIS is estimated to be 1:130,000. The data varies somewhat as estimates do but as you can see, I was born with a very rare condition.

So, what is PAIS? Well, let me share with you the full and complete 21st century understanding of Full and Partial AIS.

Without getting too technical, as this is my story and not a medical journal, I was born with a congenital birth defect, which affects the individual three times in their life. The first time it affects the person is as a fetus at seven to ten weeks of gestation. The mother begins to produce androgens, which are male sex hormones. (Now you know why expecting moms get kind of aggressive and cranky at times.) These hormones flood her body and the womb in search of the Y chromosome in the cells responsible for genitalia. In a normal XY male fetus, as the androgens enter the womb they are received into each cell by means of 'androgen receptors,' and then interact with the Y chromosome in the cells responsible for genital development. As a result of that meeting, it triggers the fetus' genitalia to go male.

In someone with full AIS, none of the androgen receptors function, so despite the androgens that the mother is producing and the Y chromosomes that are present in the fetus's cells, they never meet, and as a result, the fetus' genitals fully default to female.

In someone who has PAIS, only some of the cells have working receptors. So, as a result, the genitalia at birth can be anywhere from nearly normal male to nearly normal female, and anywhere in between depending on what cells have working receptors.

The second time it affects the individual, is at four to five months of gestation, when once again the mother floods her body and the womb with androgens.

In a normal XY fetus, the androgens enter the cells responsible for brain development as a means to set the physical makeup of the brain, i.e. the size, wiring, and ultimately, the gender identity. The androgens meet up with the Y chromosome and trigger the brain to go male.

To be clear, gender identity is one's understanding intrinsically of who they are, male or female. In essence, it's what's between your ears that determines gender identity, and not what's between their legs. For those with full AIS, their brain's cells cannot receive the androgens, and as a result, their brain fully defaults female, along with their gender identity.

With PAIS, some of the receptors function and some don't, so the fetus will randomly develop a physically male or female brain and a random gender identity.

The last time this condition affects the individual is when they enter puberty. For a typical boy the testicles he has, produce testosterone (an androgen) and enter his cells through his receptors, and meet the Y chromosomes and trigger his body's gender traits to go male.

For those who have full AIS, they are born fully female, and know themselves to be female, and live their young lives normally. In puberty, they become stunning as all their female features are amplified. Why? Because hidden in her body are undescended testicles producing massive amounts of testosterone that her body cannot use.

In anyone with excess testosterone, the body converts the unused testosterone into estrogen. So as a result, massive quantities of testosterone are converted into estrogen and introduced into her system—far more than normal—, and as a result, her beauty is amplified. The only issue for her is that she cannot have children as she is born without a uterus.

Full AIS is generally discovered, as she never menstruates, and is eventually taken to the doctor to find out why. It is then that they discover the undescended testicles, and realize that this completely normal, fully developed, and exceptionally stunning young woman, with normal female genitalia, is chromosomally male.

Welcome to the grey zone!

For those with PAIS, the individual produces the testosterone, but only some of the cells will receive it, so by the end of puberty, the individual with PAIS has an entirely random set of primary and secondary male and female gender traits and generally lower levels of testosterone and higher levels of estrogen.

The key to understanding PAIS is to understand the complete randomness of it. It is to appreciate that every person who has PAIS will have an entirely different set of male and female gender traits, random genitalia, and a random gender identity.

So, what is a gender trait?

For women, it's hip development, a smaller stature, breast development, soft rounded skin, a different fat distribution than men, as well as higher levels of fat throughout her body, a lack of significant body hair, and no facial hair.

For men, it's a protruding jaw bone, protruding eyebrow bones, an 'Adam's apple' (and a low voice as a result), a larger stature, bigger hands and feet, facial hair, more sharply defined body lines because of less fat and far more muscle generally. They are stronger, tighter, and leaner.

CHAPTER 2

THERE WAS a case not that long ago, of a seventy-three-year-old grandmother with three kids, (via adoption), nine grandkids, and a husband of forty years, who came to find out that she has full AIS, and is chromosomally male.

I remember reading an article about her, and what she went through and the shame she suddenly felt. She said the number one thing she questioned was who she was, male or female, and what she was going to do about it.

For those with full AIS, their bodies fully develop female, and except for hidden testicles, they are women in every sense of the word and know themselves to be such. Yet, despite that, at the end of the article, it said she was still trying to come to grips with this about herself, questioning if she should change her gender, divorce her husband, etc.

Imagine living your entire life as a normal, comfortable, and confident married woman and a grandmother, then coming to find out that you are chromosomally male!

I was born in 1964 with the partial version and very messed up genitalia. Add to this, that in 1964 it was the understanding that if a child was born with indeterminate genitalia, a parent could simply pick the gender they wanted, and then enforce that gender on the child, making it all about nurture and not nature. My parents, when presented with a choice, as my genitalia was quite messed up, chose to raise me male, because as my mom put it, "Boys are easier to raise than girls."

Thankfully, medical science came to fully understand this condition in the late 90s with regards to brain development. They finally debunked the 'nurture philosophy,' knowing that gender identity is 100% a product of nature, taking place in the womb as the brain develops.

Generally, now, for a newborn with PAIS, they hold off picking a gender for the child, or they choose a temporary placeholder gender until the child grows more, and the gender identity can be ascertained with reasonable assurance. Then the gender is properly set. Thankfully, they understand the randomness of this condition regarding gender identity, despite the physical genitalia that may be very much one way or the other.

So, my parents went home with a child they chose to be a boy, thinking that with proper gender enforcement like the doctors told them, I would be a regular boy. Well, to be fair to everyone, they did have a fifty-fifty shot at getting my gender correct, except for the fact that they didn't know that my brain developed female.

CHAPTER 3

My Life Before Puberty

"When I approach a child, she inspires in me two sentiments — tenderness for what she is, and respect for what she may become." - Louis Pasteur

I WANT TO START OUT this section of the book by saying that I love my parents deeply. They're both gone now but I hold nothing against them for what happened to me in this time, and I never once blamed them because they simply did the best they could.

Before her death five years ago, my mom and I finally did have the relationship we were always meant to have. It was short-lived because of her passing, but it was finally real and complete.

I also want to say, that although I'm going to focus on the negative and profoundly detrimental parts of my childhood, my life wasn't all bad. I have many fond and happy memories growing up, from tobogganing at the nearby golf course and hot chicken noodle soup when I got home, to my life at the cottage we rented every summer, spending my weekdays with just my mom and my dog. Endless nights of cards, puzzles, and comic books as the crickets chirped outside. Taking my small boat to the golf course to play a round of golf or just going fishing. Even visiting the elderly neighbours up and down the coast to play cards with them.

Part of what I'm going to describe are memories that came back to me that I pushed aside and forgot, as a means for a small child to cope. Part of it also is from speaking to my mom later in my 30s regarding what happened with my parents and the doctors.

The number one thing you must understand is that I didn't know I had PAIS until early 2013 when I was formally diagnosed with it. Not that it would have helped me in 1964, but it sure helps children who are born with it in 2017 ensure they receive the right treatment.

CHAPTER 4

A FEW YEARS AGO, I spoke to a mom on Facebook who had a five-year-old child with PAIS. She asked me when I knew I was a girl. I told her it was long before I went to school. It wasn't a conscious thing really but simply an intrinsic understanding.

She asked me so she could better understand when it was safe to permanently determine the gender of her child. They had given their infant baby a male placeholder gender but were very open to changing it. She told me they offered their child both male and female toys and would encourage the child no matter what gender toy they played with. At the time, she was pretty sure her child was a boy; he certainly acted like a boy in every way, and they were pretty sure they could rest in that.

I laughed and told her they did have a fifty-fifty chance of picking the right gender. Sadly, I did need to warn her that although he may be male in his mind and even mostly in his genitalia, at the end of puberty, he might be the most beautiful looking girl in his school.

Because, unlike being transgendered, where they can block and/or introduce gender-based hormones during puberty to change the body's gender traits to match the gender identity the person knows themselves to be, no amount of injected androgens will make a body male if most of the androgen receptors don't work. So, in the end, her five-year-old boy could default to nearly entirely female in puberty, and there's nothing that can be done about it.

Welcome to the grey zone!

For me, the number one thing I remember about the conversation was the shame she felt. The doctors told her and her husband to say nothing to anyone and to keep it to themselves. She also said that because they lived in the southern United States, they couldn't let the Christians around them know about his condition because they feared the inevitable attack on themselves and their child for a condition he was born with. She told me that if they have to change their son's gender, they had plans to move out of state and start fresh for his sake. She had previously seen Christians viciously pounce on other children and their families, and she would not let them do it to their child.

I didn't speak to that point with her, despite being a Christian myself, because I've witnessed so often that when it comes to an illness or condition involving genitalia or gender in any way, far too many Christians assume sin, believe what they want, ignore the truth, and judge without any facts. Sadly, some even self-righteously abuse viciously however they can to rid their community of a child born with a genetic condition.

But, honestly, I was just so surprised that she felt such fear and shame in 2014, despite so much understanding we now have regarding this condition that was non-existent when I was born. Why must parents still hide this? Why must they feel shame for a medical condition their child developed in the womb? And most of all, why were Christians the only group she mentioned that they feared would seek to destroy their child?

Chapter 5

"Parents need to fill a child's bucket of self-esteem so high that the rest of the world can't poke enough holes to drain it dry." - Alvin Price

MY PARENTS also told no one. Not my brothers, grandparents, friends—no one knew. My mom said that there was so much shame in my messed up genitalia that even my mom and dad didn't speak about it amongst themselves. They knew I was the way I was, and they left it at that. I was picked to be their son, and that was all that was said.

Unfortunately, by the age of three, it was very apparent to my parents that I wasn't a boy. My mannerisms, and innate gender-based actions, reactions and desires were that of a typical little girl. So they went back to the doctors for guidance, as it appeared that nurturing me to be a boy wasn't working. They were told that I was simply confused and they needed to take a firmer hand to the situation and show me I was a boy, and that it was on them, that they were completely failing me. The doctors told them I would grow up confused, and unable to cope or manage in the world if they didn't enforce my gender firmly.

So, armed with that advice, it was made known to me what was acceptable. My behaviour, likes, dislikes and desires were to be male and would be monitored, controlled, and enforced however necessary. I was, in essence, given a 'little boys do list' and a 'little boys don't list' and it was strictly enforced.

The enforcement began with verbal shaming whenever I naturally expressed myself, but it quickly progressed to physical punishment if I strayed from that list. It got to the point that around kindergarten age I remember playing dress-up in my mom's clothes in hiding. In the very early morning hours, I would sneak downstairs to the dryer and would put on her clothes and grab a pair of her heels from the storage closet.

But this too wasn't without risk because I remember panic and dread course through me as one morning the floorboards creaked above me as someone arose upstairs! I was petrified that someone would come downstairs and see me dressed in my mom's clothes. I remember vividly the adrenalin rushing through me and the absolute fear that overwhelmed me as I stood still like a statue. I knew if I was caught, the beating would be extreme. Even for my young mind, I knew that despite the joy in being myself, and the joy of play, the risk of dress-up was huge. I even went to great lengths to make sure that everything I took was exactly the way I found it, in case someone would notice something was out of place.

Looking back, it's so sad that instead of being celebrated as the little girl I was, and encouraged to express myself, they were trying at all costs to shame and beat the girl out of me.

I remember in kindergarten I only wanted to play with the girls and do the girl activities. The teacher would grab me by the arm and take the doll I was feeding from my hands and put me down to the floor with the boys playing with the blocks. Yet, I would quickly migrate back to the girls and the task of feeding my baby.

I remember after several attempts to put me with the boys, she asked me why I didn't want to play with them. I told her I wanted to feed my baby. In the end, she gave up despite her attempts to force a gender-based play choice on me.

By the first grade, however, things changed for me. At home, I spent most of my time in hiding or I went outside. Even in the dead of winter, I would bundle up and go outside and just sit in the snow for hours to escape the shaming and physical pain.

Looking back, the reason I hid was that no matter what I did or said, they would see it as female and try to beat it out of me. My life became one of fear, abuse, desperation, and loneliness in my own home, and ultimately at school as well.

I remember one day in the first grade doing a craft with the kids around me when it dawned on me that I wasn't one of them. I didn't belong there. I didn't belong anywhere. It was the day I realized I was in the grey zone.

I knew I was an outsider in a class full of boys and girls. I wasn't like the boys, despite my outward appearance, and I wasn't like the girls because I wasn't allowed to express myself as one.

I avoided the boys because they were violent and mean to me, and the girls avoided me because I didn't look like them; so I played alone.

I learned it was safest to be a loner, separate, and self-sufficient and it became my life. I began to keep to myself, and I said little to anyone out of great fear, and I kept a very low profile at home and at school. I would spend most recesses away from everyone in the far corners of the playground. I learned that the only safe place was when I was alone.

I also became very angry, jealous, and resentful of the girls. Picture day was for me a profoundly jealous and bitter day. The girls would come in their pretty dresses, tights, Mary-Janes, and long lovely hair with beautiful ribbons, and I would stare at them desperate to be one of them. I longed to be loved and celebrated as the little girl I was and longed most of all to just be myself.

It was a difficult time for me knowing intrinsically who I was but not being allowed to express it. I was angry, and yet I didn't know how to deal with it.

Love from my parents had become entirely conditional on how well I put my true self down and pretended to be what my parents told me to be. When I pretended well, I was loved, but I would inevitably slip and express myself and suffer at their hands for it.

In the end, my sense of self was lost as I pushed it to the side to cope and survive. At a very young age, I put my true identity into the realm of the impossible. In turn, I gave up hope and entered into a place of complete surrender, sadness, and despair as I grew to embrace the false persona of my parents' design. Yet looking back, I now know that they never made me a boy—they just made me a non-girl.

What was so ethically criminal about this time was that they told me that who I am at my core was wrong, and that they would tell me who I was. Having someone in absolute power in your life telling you daily to feel shame about yourself at your deepest levels permanently damaged me! I was made to feel worthless and dirty. Nothing about me was celebrated, loved, or encouraged. Everything I did was a source of shame, guilt, and ridicule. It was never about me doing wrong; I was told every day that I, myself, was wrong and a mistake.

Imagine telling your four-year-old daily that you don't like them, and daily shaming and abusing them for what they say and do. Imagine what would happen to that poor little soul in a very short time. They would be broken, lost, and destitute of hope, with nowhere to run or hide, nowhere to know love, and never to know the touch of a loving hand.

They would live in constant fear, and would not even be old enough to comprehend why they are being beaten.

My parents, over time, had destroyed my spirit and made me feel worthless. With no self-worth or self-esteem, I lost myself and my true identity and just began an aimless existence, destitute of life within me.

By the age of seven, I was taken to the hospital because I had such constant pains in my stomach, they thought I had an ulcer. What seven-year-old has an ulcer! Yet, no one looked for an emotional source for the sadness and anxiety I felt that was manifesting itself in my body in such an acute way. In the end, they just accepted that I had a nervous stomach and left it at that.

Between the ages of seven and twelve, I escaped my life through television, and I found love in food. I wasn't physically hiding around the house so much because I had knuckled under and had given up hope. They had beaten me down and brainwashed me to be what they told me to be. I became an expert at playing the part they had laid out for me, despite the sadness and emptiness inside me that never abated.

By the age of twelve, I was watching eight hours of television a day and weighed over 200 pounds. Television was huge for me. I would fall into the dramas and become the people in those shows. My favourite show was *Little House on the Prairie.* I loved Melissa Gilbert, and I identified with her. Watching Laura Ingles face her challenges, and yet, having a mother and father who loved her, made me feel as if every week I too was in Walnut Grove.

For an hour a week I found escape and belonging, and in many ways they became my true family growing up.

People have asked me over the years how I came to choose Laura as my new name. It's because of this time and the happiness and escape it afforded me. The name 'Laura' represented hope in my young life. It was the only show that swept me away into a safe and loving place. I knew it wasn't real, but dreaming of an unreal television love was better than my reality.

Scholastically I suffered greatly. I didn't learn to read until I was eight and struggled with school including failing grade six. I was so abused and brainwashed it's no wonder I was failing school. I was deeply distracted and detached from reality and didn't care. There were fun times and good days, but most of the time, it was as if I was watching my life through a television. I had resigned from life at my core. Nothing for me mattered or made sense anymore. I was sad, confused, and really fat. I felt ugly and distant from everything and everyone.

So as puberty neared, the worst part of PAIS was about to begin.

Part 2

From Puberty to My Awakening

Chapter 6

"When people are emotionally isolated, they keep their feelings completely to themselves, are unable to receive emotional support from others, feel "shut down" or numb, and are reluctant or unwilling to communicate with others, except perhaps for the most superficial matters." – goodtherapy.org

IMAGINE as you entered grade nine, the abuse you would suffer for being a short, massively overweight boy, with no social skills, large developing breasts, a feminine voice, round soft skin, the fat distribution of a girl, female legs, no facial or body hair, a feminine face and voice. Imagine the shame, desperation, and abuse and having no support from anyone.

I was trying to cope with all of the above, but all I did was eat more and watch more television to escape further. The older girls would tell me to get a bra as they laughed at me in the hallway. Eventually, I learned to wear a light jacket at all times so my breasts would be covered up. I hated myself, and I felt so ugly and confused; I was an unwanted and abused misfit.

By grade 10, they decided to take me to the hospital to run tests because I had no male gender traits at all. It was determined that I had normal teenage hormone levels for a girl! Yet, did they stop and wonder why? Did they consider that perhaps there was more to it? Nope. They ignored it all, and pressed forward hoping as the doctor said that, 'things would right themselves in time.'

Also in this period, the shame I felt mounted. Phys Ed class became the worst for me. I would be made to strip from the waist up and bare my breasts for everyone to see. They were so large and beautiful that the girls would crowd around the windows of the gym to watch me and laugh. The fact that I needed to get a bra became 'the comment.' So, ultimately, I just pulled away further from everyone and did what is written at the top of the chapter. I was friendless and feared everyone. I learned to hide in plain sight and not bring light on myself at all. I learned to be invisible, say little, and blend into the background.

People knew me, but I was an independent. I was a loner and was so damaged that it's a wonder I didn't try to kill myself back then. I was just so good at escaping into my safe place that it eased the pain, fear, isolation, and the knowledge that I was a freak and unloved. I was a wash of hormones and feelings that were a jumbled mess, and I was now so conditioned to only feel and react as a male, and yet, everything about my body was screaming female!

The one thing I most struggled with from an early age was not being allowed to cry. I was desperate to cry, but that wasn't allowed in my reality of my parents making. I learned that I had to bury my feelings and emotions until they came out in inappropriate ways, then I was punished for that too. I was never given, as girls get, the opportunity to work through my feelings freely, including tears, and talk them out and learn to express them in a healthy way.

I find it extremely rare to meet a wife who doesn't comment about her husband's inability to express emotions well. Society wonders why men cannot express themselves in a healthy way! That's because growing up they aren't allowed to. They have to shove it all down, keep silent, suck it up, and be a man. That's all they were taught by older men who are as inept at expressing emotions as they are. It's no wonder that when a man gets angry, instead of having the tool and skills learned growing up to cope and deal with it in a healthy way like his wife, he winds up doing or saying something foolish and shortsighted.

I also had a very delicate soft feminine spirit; something else boys aren't allowed to have. Yet, over the decades, and the abuse I suffered, it took until the fall of 2016 for me to rediscover within myself that delicate feminine spirit I used to have.

By the age of fifteen, things weren't 'righting themselves,' and my breasts were as beautiful, full, and pretty as any of the girls in my class. And, except for my hips not widening, my body was female. Yet, instead of stopping the madness, and re-examining the choice they made regarding my gender when I was an infant, revisiting the tests done a year earlier, or even talking to me about it, or taking me to a psychologist, my parents instead, took me to the hospital and had my breasts gutted out of my chest, taking all the glandular tissues as well so they couldn't grow back.

Eight hundred stitches and over five hours later, they left me with two massive scars on my chest.

If I could afford to put them back, I would, but it's just so expensive. I've come to a place of accepting this condition, but I sincerely yearn to have my breasts again.

They were mine, and they took them from me! My breasts were the one major female gender trait that I did have, and I tear up knowing that I will never have them back, not the way they were.

Chapter 7

BY MY EARLY twenties I was profoundly lost, confused, friendless, and completely isolated. I never dated—who would want to be with me? I was a fat ugly freak, not male or female. I had developed some male traits in my early twenties, like a larger stature, the loss of my hair but gaining of some facial hair instead. Yet, in nearly all the other gender traits, I was female except for hip development.

My God, I was so confused!

I had no one, and I was so lost. I think the only reason I could cope, was that I had been living in misery for so long that I had become used to it, and I found ways to cope through television and food. I had acquaintances but no deep friendships and no understanding as to why I was so sad and lost inside. I just knew that I would spend the rest of my life absolutely alone.

At twenty-three I moved out of my parents' home to live alone as a hollow shell of a person - a persona with no substance. I was a façade - a phony. I was just so good at playing the part given to me that I didn't know there was anything else.

At twenty-nine I hit my emotional wall, and I tried to kill myself. I hanged myself from a hook that was rated to hold 600 pounds of weight.

There's no doubt in my mind that I went to hell for a time. It was absolute black with no light and completely void of God and hope. I felt a penetrating chilling cold like the cold you get in your bones laying on cold marble on a hot summer day. But worst of all, it was a permanent place of never-ending suffering. There are no words to describe the terror

I endured. It was 'nothingness' to me, and as I lingered there, I realized it was stone cold permanent, and there was no way out! I was destined to suffer forever in a void of agonizing separation from God because I made a horrible mistake.

Then the hook broke! By God's grace, it broke! Rated to hold something weighing 600 pounds and despite me weighing only 240 pounds, it broke!! In time, I fought to wake harder than ever before to live and escape being permanently put there.

Eventually when I came to I began to shake violently as the panic and absolute terror lingered for hours after. Despite how sad, lonely, and void of hope I felt, I knew that a place far worse awaited me if I ever tried that again!

Chapter 8

A T THIRTY-ONE, I came to Christ on a fledgling thing called the internet and went from being alone in a basement room one Sunday to being at church for the first time in my life the following Sunday.

It was a Sunday morning in February 1996 when I got on the internet, and I happened upon the IRC chat lines.

It was basically several thousand channels where people can talk. The subject usually related to the title of the channel. So as I went from one channel to another, of the over 5000 thousands channels, a persistent guy began to harass me. I didn't want to leave the network, but I needed to get away from this guy. Yet, no matter what channel I entered, he would follow me into the channel, then private message me lewd comments. In desperation, and with thousands of channels to choose from, and with the names of the channels scrolling by very quickly on my screen, I entered 'Christian Singles.'

Immediately, I noticed that he didn't follow me there. I asked if I could hang out there, even though I wasn't a Christian, explaining that this pervert was following me. They made me feel very welcome, and they didn't try to shove Christianity down my throat as someone I knew did when I was a teenager.

I avoided Christians at this point because they were represented by the guys in white suits on Sunday TV who came with empty promises and in search of stupid people to hand them their money. You know the type, "Get a prayer towel for $69.95 and we'll throw in a free lapel pin that says, 'I really am that stupid.' We're doing the Lord's work here, and oh, by the way, my driver tells me that Rolls Royce number four needs a tune-up, so don't delay in sending me, um I mean God your money."

I'm being hard I know, but that's how I saw it.

As far as the chat line, there's a process where you type in the main board area but can also have private message windows as well where you can have private conversations with individual users on the channel. So as message after message scrolled by on the main board, I was contacted privately by a person whose handle was 'wn14jsus.' (win one for Jesus) To be honest, I read it as, 'win fourteen jsus'. Sad, I know but what can I say!

Her name was Wendy, and she was a student at Cal State in San Lois Obispo, California. Over the day, we talked about lots of things. She would ask me my opinion about religion and such. I told her about this person shoving it down my throat, and she was surprisingly understanding. When she left for church in the early afternoon (my time), I remember how much I needed her. I remember that it was the longest few hours waiting for her return. She had, unbeknownst to me, become a lifeline for me.

She did eventually return, and as the day became evening, I began to cry as we spoke. I was so lost and desperately lonely, yet she stood by me for most of the day. I was leaning on a young woman 4000 miles away, and she was there for me when I needed someone the most. I came to find out that she put her hectic schedule on hold that day for me.

Finally, I got to the one question that was at the heart of my terror. I asked her, "If I take Jesus into my heart, will I go to nothingness?"

"No, you'll be with Jesus in heaven," was her reply.

I asked, "Can I ask the others on the main board?"

"Sure," she said. "Just let me quiet things down in there first."

Appreciate that this channel was very silly, and the people on it were equally silly. It wasn't a serious channel at all, no apologetic debates, just relaxation, banter and fun. So, she typed in the main board, and told everyone to be quiet, and that I had a serious question to ask everyone. Amazingly, and instantly, everyone shut up, and the channel went silent.

Then, one message after another from everyone appeared on the board, "What's your question?"

What's my question? I was stunned at the love I was feeling. They dropped everything, all twenty-five of them, to focus on me! With tears rolling down my cheeks I typed, "If I accept Jesus into my heart will I go to nothingness?"

I waited for a response. Then, like nothing I ever experienced before, I began to see the same exact answer come across the board from one person after another: "No. You will be with Jesus in heaven." Consider that people all over the world were typing those exact same words at the exact same time! The exact same words!

At that moment, I chose to accept Jesus into my life, and I distinctly felt three jolts to my body. Here I was alone in my room in a basement of a house, and I was getting mysteriously jolted. I told Wendy about being jolted, and she said that it was the Holy Spirit.

I responded, "The Holy what?"

Well, that night I decided to make a commitment. For me, it was like a pledge on a telethon. You pledge the money, and in a few days, the envelope comes. I made the pledge to follow Christ, but I didn't really know what that meant, or why I wasn't feeling it in my heart but just in my mind. I had resolved to believe, but that was all. In the Bible, Acts chapter 8 talks about this, taking the name of Christ but not having the Holy Spirit yet; that was me.

The next day, there was a freak ice storm that hit the city that made the roads impassable. I stayed home from work and went back to Christian Singles. Several people, who were present the night before began to ask me the nagging question: "Got a church yet? Got a church yet?" Oh, they never gave up asking me that question. I told them politely to give me some space. I needed time to process what had happened to me.

By the next day, I was being asked again. So, out of desperation, I finally agreed to find a church, so into the yellow pages I went. Yes, I know, the yellow pages. For you millennials, think of it as a book form of Google for businesses.

I took suggestions from this guy who was there on Sunday night and eventually decided on a church, and I went there that Sunday. Three months to the day that I met Wendy online, I was baptized. Then when I came out of the water for the first time in my life, the Holy Spirit came upon me!

I felt so silly and giddy. I remember sitting in the front row listening to the sermon thinking, I have absolutely no idea what he's saying, but I'm sure it's good. It was an exciting time for me as a new believer, and for a time the sadness abated somewhat. God filled my heart and soul with his presence and brought loving people into my life who really cared about me. I was overwhelmed with my connection to the Holy Spirit, and so excited and hopeful.

I remember being invited to lunch at the home of an older couple in the church. As we ate lunch, they kept grinning at me. Eventually, I asked them why and they told me that they loved having new Christians around because they're always on fire and excited about God; it kept them young. I was learning so much about him and this new way of living and thinking. I had arrived in him, and yet, I was still very lost within myself.

A year later, I met a twenty-year-old woman who was more mixed up emotionally than I was. She was suffering from an undiagnosed serious mental health condition, and like me, she too was desperate for love and stability.

After a few months, we married. She knew I was useless to her in bed, yet in time, she came to understand that I was useless to her in every way. She was looking to me for the innate things which only a genuine man could provide. Yet, even though I was playing the part of a man, I wasn't one, and I had absolutely no ability to satisfy her needs and provide for her something innately male that I didn't possess. After three years together we split and ultimately divorced.

She told me at our last encounter in the fall of 2004 that I was a woman and that I wasn't a guy at all. She then asked me if I had ever considered it. This was a profound question! It was as if she asked me the golden key of all questions, which would unlock the reason for everything bad in my life to that point—the sadness and my feelings of being so incomplete. She reminded me of the existence of a truth that I once knew as a small child, which I had long ago placed way off to the side of my mind as an impossibility never to attain.

But not only did she ask me, she made it clear that my being a woman was my truth and my reality. Despite my best efforts to be male I failed, because I wasn't one and I needed to consider her determination that I was a woman. She had lived closely with me for several years. Who knows you better than your spouse?

It triggered my awakening. Her comments that day would ultimately bring me home to the truth of who I was all along, and who I was always meant to be.

From 2005 to June of 2007 three major things were going on at the same time. Up until now, this book has been quite linear as we've moved through the years of my life but I want to separate these two years and discuss three things separately: My rebirth, my time in God's boot camp and my church life. They are all unique, and although they do intersect, I want to discuss them on their own.

My Rebirth

Chapter 9

THIS PORTION of my story is very personal to me. I cannot begin to tell you the trepidation I feel in exposing myself by writing it down. My life before and during this time has always been very private for me. In this section of the book, I'm going to share my personal journey in my rebirth that happened over the two plus years that followed my parting from my ex and my moving back to Toronto.

No one has ever heard this part of my story. I skim over it when I've shared my story with others, but I think it's time to get into the specifics and the mechanics of what I felt and did in this time.

Despite my ex's statement to me that I was a woman, at the time I wasn't sure this was the right course of action. The memories of my childhood had yet to surface, yet I knew her comment had struck home to me in an incredibly deep way, and I knew I needed to try her suggestion.

Unfortunately, my body without my breasts was far more male. I have all the secondary female gender traits but now none of the primary ones, so I set out to find a shop in Toronto to help me.

Thinking back now it was rather funny as I went into this fetish shop that contained the wildest items to help guys become women. Outlandish wigs and black 6" stiletto heels in massive shoe sizes and so many wild fetish items. It was really bizarre, and I felt so strange being there, not really knowing what I was doing but just going on instinct.

I told the sales woman, "I just want to look like the nice girl next door," and I explained that I was there exploring my identity and nothing else.

I'm glad I met her because she really understood. I went from nervous and unsure to the opposite. She commented about my many physical female attributes and said that it would be easy to help me, 'be that nice girl next door,' because I was already most of the way there.

In time I had purchased all I needed and went home to try it all out.

When I finally put everything on and looked in the mirror, I began to cry. I don't think many of you reading this can possibly find a frame of reference to what I'm about to write. It's so natural for you, so real to you that you can't possibly appreciate these next words. But when I looked at myself in the mirror, out of my mouth and through the tears, I began to repeat these words, over and over: "My God it's me. It's me!"

For the first time in my life, I wasn't looking at a stranger, I was looking at myself in the mirror. My outward appearance matched my inward self! I was pretty and beautiful; all the things I was on the inside that my parents took from me. I was finally, for the first time in my life outwardly the woman I was always meant to be. It's as if the last two pieces of the jigsaw puzzle of my life, had been found that day and placed in the puzzle. Now for the first time, I was looking at the complete picture. Things made sense, and I finally felt right and complete.

To see my reflection and knowing that my outward reflection matched me on the inside! I know that's a hard concept so let me try to help you.

Appreciate that when you meet a person, they see you physically, and hear your voice and treat you male or female. If you look like a woman, they relate to you as one. But when you are made to dress as a man and are forced to fake it, women treat you as one and automatically change how they relate to you.

Over the years I've come to see that women change quite a bit in that. Women subconsciously see men as adversaries, an 'us versus them' mentality. With other women, women let their guard down and treat each other more like a vast sisterhood of comradery and support. Women tend to stick together, and they talk in ways men cannot fathom. Yet when men are around, women tend to be far more reserved and basic in their speech. It's not a clinical trial or relational bias on my part but my experience as one who related to them from both sides of the fence. I was treated very differently.

I know that I would make the most fantastic marriage counsellor. I can talk guy, and I can understand the intricacies and nuances of girl speak. I relate to both genders because I was raised one and born another so I can appreciate both sides because I lived both sides.

For my girlfriends I can explain her husband to her, and what he's thinking since he never communicates with her. For him, I can share what she expects and needs from him, which he's totally clueless to know on his own, despite her 5000 hints - some very plain.

I personally think that every married man needs one solid female friend to help him navigate the massively intricate sensitivities, feelings, and demands that his wife expects of him. And I think every wife needs one solid guy friend to help her understand that she needs to speak to her husband slowly and not expect him to pick up on even obvious clues she leaves. If her speech is not direct, open and to the point in less than twenty words, you will lose him. And no hinting! Be short, direct, and straight up; it's all he understands and appreciates.

Okay, now back to my story.

I did eventually go out that afternoon, but I'm not sure how well I did. I know that statement makes no sense, but you have to understand that I had played the lie of male for so long! I was made to walk like one and act like one, mimicking so many subtle male traits from before kindergarten that I didn't yet know how to let it all go and just be myself.

The natural me had been bound and hidden for so long that like a butterfly coming out of its cocoon, where it needs a lot of time for its wings to expand and dry out, I too needed time to work this all out and come out of my cocoon. It took three to five years of brainwashing by my parents and decades of perfecting this lie. Then in one afternoon I finally threw it all down and saw it for the lie it was.

It was the day I woke from my nightmare.

Yet, what was next for me? I may have identified my true self as female, but I had no way of knowing who I truly was or what this meant for me moving forward. I had buried my true self when I was a small child, and it was going to take a lot of time to find myself again and discover who I was and who I wanted to be.

In fact, it took a full year to parse out the true me from the false persona; identifying the things I liked to do because I was conditioned to like them, from the things I truly liked or wanted to do or try.

Like exploring the many things denied to me and now allowing myself the opportunity to have them. Like taking ballet class in pink tights and a leotard and piercing my ears. These were things I had always wanted to do but were denied. Wearing tights and a pretty skirt to church and just enjoying the freedom of being the woman I was. Finally having the right to choose what I wore, skirts or pants, was so freeing. I was so excited going clothes shopping in the women's section of the department store and not feeling fear but rather acceptance from those around me and knowing in my core that I belonged there all along.

The freedom of this time was beyond words for me.

As with a butterfly taking flight for the first time, it was a time for me to emotionally dance and express myself, and to celebrate who I was! It was the most exciting time of my life. The only word to best describe how I felt was 'glee.'

I was finally discovering who I was without anyone interfering. I was seen and treated as the woman I am as women were relating to me as a woman. I was free and exploring myself, and I enjoyed my femininity without fear, shame, or guilt for the first time in my life.

Yet, it was actually a difficult time for me as well, because I was still living a double life. In the evening and on the weekends, including church, I was free to be myself, but at work, I was still expected to be the fake guy. This went on for the better part of a year until one Monday in the late summer of 2006 I couldn't bear to pretend any longer.

So that day I approached one of the Christian owners and explained to them that I was a woman and that I had to be who I was all along, and that come the following Monday I would begin to visit their office as myself. They promptly terminated my contract and begged me to seek help.

Ultimately, terminating my contract was the best thing that could have happened for me because that day I was officially and permanently me, full-time. I saw my doctor and proceeded to fill out the paperwork to change my name.

Also in this time, I got in touch with some of my Christian friends from California I knew when I lived there as a guy. I had shared with them my change and their reaction was so surprising to me.

All six already knew I was female. They saw I wasn't male, despite my conditioning to be one. The husband of the office manager I worked with told me that he heard me speak and he said to me, "I thought to myself, you weren't male, and you weren't a gay male either. Actually, you sounded just like my wife."

The office manager commented to me that she and I would talk at my desk at the office over tea before work daily, and as she thought about it, she realized that we were having a hen party every morning. She said no other guy would ever do that and she loved that about me.

It's important that you remember their reactions to me. These Christians knew me when I was pretending to be male, yet they saw right through it. They knew and understood that this change was correct for me and that the lie of my life was trying to be something my parents and the doctors decided. I never decided to be a woman in my late 30's, I already was one! My only decision was to let go of the lie.

There was one thing left that I had to do—I had to inform my brothers and sit down with my mom. After many years of suffering from dementia, my father had passed, so it was just my mom that I needed to see.

Chapter 10

My Dad

I HAVEN'T MENTIONED my dad much up till now, and I wanted to devote a chapter to him.

My father was a good man, and I know he deeply loved me. We spent time together when I was younger, but not as much as my mom and me.

He tried, that's all I know.

When I moved back to the area in late 2004, his dementia was progressing. I stayed with my parents for two weeks before my apartment became available and I had a chance to spend time with him. He was only about 40% himself at that point, but he did have many lucid moments. This time was truly a gift from God because only three weeks later he had a massive stroke and was gone mentally after that.

I will always be proud of my dad. He was a wireless-air gunner on a Lancaster bomber in WWII from 1944-45 flying sorties over Germany. Yet, what I most remember about him was the pottery he began in our basement that turned into a thriving business. I remember as a peewee my dad would push the packed boxes out of the way so I could ride my tricycle around the glazing table because they were too heavy for me to push myself.

I find his pottery online from time to time, yet I have but one piece. In fact, some of his pottery now rests in several museums. I think he would be so honored knowing that. He made complete dinner sets and so much more, dozens of styles of mugs and plates etc. all highly sought after for the amazingly colourful and imaginative glazes he used. (On my website there are some pictures of my dad and his work.

(www.livinglifeinthegreyzone.com)

On Fridays, when I was around six or so, he would pick me up from school and take me to get junk food from the grocery store, pork ribs for his toaster oven, and always Kraft onion BBQ Sauce for those ribs. He'd set me up a spot on his workbench with a sleeping bag. Then I'd hang out with him watching TV as he tended to the kilns. These are the fondest memories I have of him. My only regret was not staying with him. After a time, probably around nine p.m., I'd go up and watch TV with my mom. I remember him gently begging me to stay, crestfallen that his time with me was over and too short for him. He never stopped me, but I know now how sad he was when I left. He'd come up with some ribs for me later, but I always sensed that he wished I had stayed with him.

What I would do to just stay with him once more!

What I miss most is his advice. I was too young and stupid to appreciate much of what he told me. Much of it was about the work world. He was a true renaissance man. He had jobs from selling cars to women's shoes and clothes, to being a master at virtually every building trade there is, including building the home I grew up in. It's in the Renaissance of him that I take after him the most. I too am very similar in that regard.

My father wasn't perfect. He drank a lot and was loose with the money, and most of all, he loved the toys. Boats, snowmobiles; you name it, he had it. And, as my mom always said referring to him, no doubt, "The only difference between men and boys is the price of their toys."

That was my dad. I miss you, dad. You were a good man, I love you so much.

Chapter 11

IT WAS THE fall of 2006, and I went up to see my mom. I sat down with her and I shared what I needed to do for myself, and that I would legally be Laura very soon.

I expected resistance from her. I expected her to try to convince me to remain the way I was, and yet, my mom began to cry. But they weren't tears of fear or panic; they were tears of immense guilt.

To truly appreciate my mom you need to know that she grew up in the Depression to parents of Scottish descent. She learned to keep a stiff upper lip and never cry! Yet, that day she wept as the guilt poured out of her. It was also to be the day that I learned about my days as an infant and the decisions that were made regarding my gender.

Most of what I relayed earlier in the book came from this conversation. She said that she knew deep down I wasn't a boy and that they had picked wrong and that the doctors were wrong in their advice and I was simply being myself.

I asked her why she let the farce go on. She pleaded with me that the doctors were pushing them to see it through, but also, it was the sixties, and you didn't change the gender of a child. She told me that my condition was the greatest guilt and shame she had ever known in her life. All the more reinforced when she came to see my true female gender develop but chose to do as the doctors instructed her to do to me.

I asked her that if she knew I was a girl, then why did she let them gut my chest and take my breasts? She told me that I appeared to have embraced my male gender and that everyone felt it appropriate to remove my breasts given my sex.

What could I really say?

I wrote early that I never held my parents accountable for what they did. None of it was their fault. They were unwilling participants in this whole affair, and they did the best they could. They loved me, but because of the advice of the medical establishment, they thought they were doing the right thing. I know they never meant to hurt me directly. They thought they were helping me, and in the end, how could I be angry with two people trying the best they could under untenable circumstances. There was no malice nor premeditation to any of what happened. It was just two people who grew up during the Great Depression trying to cope the best they could, with their child having a condition requiring 21st-century medical understanding.

Yet, as I look back at my childhood as a result of that day with her, I began to realize how different I was from the rest of my brothers, and how different she treated me. I always thought it was because I was the baby of the family. I suppose that played a part, but the choice of things she and I did together were very different from what she did with my brothers. She and I were inseparable, especially at the cottage. I think she acknowledged, in subtle ways that I was her daughter, perhaps subconsciously for her after a certain point, but we did have a special bond that in time strengthened in a huge way after this conversation, as our new and real relationship was finally able to grow naturally.

It was a rough day for both of us, but it paved a way for me to permanently become the person I was always meant to be.

Yet, it was still hard for her. She had called me by a name for many decades that was about to be replaced, and she was quite old. It was hard for her to stop using it, even years later. But, even in that, I knew it wasn't intentional or malicious because she would always correct herself and apologize. I was never mad about that either; I gave her much grace. It would also take her time to get used to having a daughter. Like me shaking free of the male façade, it would take time for her to unlearn so much about me that wasn't real. My mom had to get to know me all over again. Her son was gone, but he was being replaced by her authentic and whole daughter. Much for her to embrace and accept. I gave her lots of time, and to be honest, she needed it.

My only regret was that I lived abroad most of my years prior to her passing, so I saw her very infrequently. We talked on the phone often, and they were wonderful conversations. She had a sharp and dry wit that I adored. I did fly home to spend a week with her just prior to her passing in 2012. It was a special time and one that I will always cherish.

During my visit with her, I had gone to the supermarket and saw carnations. Her room was stark and bare of any life. She had a lovely home, but her room needed colour. I purchased four or five bunches of carnations, and while she was asleep, I put them all over her room. Not only did they look beautiful; full of colour and life but they smelled so good.

Eventually, she woke and commented about the carnations and wondered who brought them. I told her that I did. She then said to me, "You know carnations are my favourite flower."

I responded, "Mine too."

Then we spoke at the same time, a sentence that summed up our relationship: "Because they last so long."

Neither of us knew our favourite flower, and yet we both loved carnations for the same practical reason.

I often say that I am my mother's daughter. Despite being nurtured to be a son I gained much of who I am from her. We both laughed when we came to find that out about each other, helping to bridge another gap of understanding between us.

It was bittersweet, however, because a few days later I had to bend over and kiss my frail and weak mom goodbye, knowing that it would be the last time I would ever see her.

People have asked me if she was saved. I don't think she was. However, I did write a fiction novel Called Rachael's Quest and sent an early manuscript to her six months before her death. In it, the gospel is preached, so perhaps she was.

There's a funny story about her and this manuscript. About a month after I sent her a hard copy I got a call. When I answered, I heard, "You killed them off!"

Not a, 'Hello sweetie how are you, it's your mama.' No, her first words were a shout.

I said, "Yes."

"You killed them off, why did you do that!"

I had killed off two characters in my book that you would have really gotten to know and love, and their deaths would have come very unexpectedly and as a complete shock to those reading the book.

I responded, "Well, none of us know how long we have, and we should never take those in our life for granted. We need to cherish them because they could be gone tomorrow."

There was this pause as she contemplated my words and then I hear her response. It was much more subdued as the wind had been taken out of her sails, "Well, you shouldn't have killed them off."

I was deeply flattered by the call, to be honest. In grade twelve I was told by my English teacher never to write a book. Well, Mrs Buckerfield, this one's for you!

I learned to read late, and really struggled with English all through school. It was the work world and writing business letters, and many hundreds of hours writing my novel that made me a better writer. Ultimately, it comes down to paying your dues. For writing, it's in the doing, not taking classes that makes you better.

My mom was an avid reader, reading two 800-page novels a week for as long as I knew her. She was gifted in English. I remember she found nineteen spelling errors in a K-Mart flyer.

So, for this woman who read thousands of big fat novels, to call me up screaming said something. My book had drawn her into my story and characters and then drew out of her such intense emotions that she had to call me up and yell at me for it. I was flattered!

I've thought about that a lot. In the publishing world, they want 'show' not 'tell.' That means you cannot say that Mr Brown has a cold. You have to show the reader by writing two giant boring descriptive paragraphs explaining all his symptoms so in the end, the reader figures that out for themselves.

Well, that's not me. I'm a storyteller, not a story 'show-er.' I've tried to consider why I'm the storyteller I am. I've spoken to more than one editor who told me I have a rare gift. They all said that being a storyteller is a gift you cannot learn; you have it or you don't.

I thought about this, and I think I got this 'gift' because of my massive imagination. Playing alone as a child for so many years, you develop a means to cope, that in turn develops into a vivid imagination, where the isolation becomes an avenue to dream and discover in your mind. A place to create stories and people, and adventures in play because there's no one to contribute, share in it, or get in the way.

At the end of this book is a short story I wrote so you can get a taste of my writing. Also, I will be releasing my novel that my mom read, on September 28th, 2017 in honor of my mom's birthday.

Find it here. www.livinglifeinthegreyzone.com

Since 2005, I was learning and growing in regard to my true gender for almost a year before I went full-time. I also spent eighty hours getting electrolysis on my face to rid myself of some of my facial hair. Yet she never finished the hair removal. I couldn't do it. Going from freedom to forcing myself back into that lie for work proved too much for me. So, as the fall of 2006 came, I was now myself full-time and with a new name.

Unfortunately, I was unable to find work, and in time my savings ran out, and since I was self-employed I was ineligible for UI, so eventually I was forced to seek welfare to survive. My very kind current landlord and his wife gave me two months free rent through the fall, but they were in the process of selling the building. Once they did, the new landlord kicked me out of my flat immediately because I still had no job.

In late 2006, I ended up in a small basement room in the middle of one of the distant suburbs of Toronto. After my rent, phone, and dial-up internet were paid, I was left with $40 a month for food. There was no food bank for me because I lived in such an isolated area.

The church I was still attending in my old neighborhood wouldn't help me. The associate pastor who ran the food bank in my church, after my second trip to use it, told me that I was cut off and I needed to find a job.

I'm not sure what he thought I was doing all day at home. I was so desperate to find work that I had enrolled in a job training course that taught people how to find employment. I spent over eight hours a day creating personalized cover letters, at least four a day, to add to my personalized resume for each job application; yet, I never did get a job.

I was free to be myself, but I was trapped in a basement with virtually no physical contact with anyone for over six months. I was alone in nearly every way, with no resources at all and slowly starving. Despite my stretching the $40 as best as I could, it only gave me about twenty or so days' worth of barley soup, the other days I didn't eat. It was the most economical food I found that I could make, and I ate it as my only meal for months.

In all that I've written so far, I haven't really talked much about my faith journey. God was very much in all that was happening to me in this time.

For this next part of my story, I want to share with you where I was in my fiath walk and all that God showed me during this time. There was to be a spiritual rebirth that awaited me, as well as God finally and profoundly taking hold of my life and my heart for good.

Part 3

Growing up Laura

Welcome to God's Boot Camp

Chapter 12

"Purify me from my sins, and I will be clean; wash me, and I will be whiter than snow. Oh, give me back my joy again; you have broken me— now let me rejoice. Don't keep looking at my sins. Remove the stain of my guilt. Create in me a clean heart, O God. Renew a loyal spirit within me. Do not banish me from your presence, and don't take your Holy Spirit from me. Restore to me the joy of your salvation, and make me willing to obey you." Psalms 51:7-12NLT

ELEVEN YEARS had passed since that Sunday and my encounter with Wendy in California who led me to Christ. Yet, my walk was far from committed. I wasn't a dedicated or serious Christian taking my walk seriously and appreciating the gift of my salvation. I was still sinning as if I wasn't saved at all.

I knew the Bible and I said all the right things on the outside, yet on the inside, I was still a liar, a manipulator, and a thief. I acted like a Christian, but I was just like one of the Pharisees that Jesus said this to: *"You are like whitewashed tombs, which look beautiful on the outside but on the inside are full of the bones of the dead and everything unclean." Matthew 23:27b NIV*

I wasn't a baby Christian either; I was far more mature than that. I was more like a rebellious teenager who was failing at school but not because I was unable to succeed but because I wasn't taking my studies seriously, and goofing off far more than I studied. Yet, God had big plans for me. It was time for me to learn about him the hard way.

In the late fall of 2006, he enlisted me in 'God's boot camp.'

He had led me to this small room in the suburbs that I rarely left. It was a prison cell in almost every way. He removed everyone out of my life that I sought comfort from and began weaning me off the world. The dependence on food and TV to cope and survive that I had leaned on for decades were completely removed from me. Instead, he began to show me himself.

In December, my journey to him truly began when I was speaking on the phone with a woman I had met on a chat line. She asked me a question that would set me on a new path. "Laura, if Jesus knocked on your door and entered your home, would he be pleased with what he saw?"

Over the years, I've learned in my Christian walk that unless the Holy Spirit is convicting you through the words being spoken by others, their words will fall short of our hearts. In other words, you can tell someone they're sinning until your lips fall off but unless God's conviction is in your words, they won't heed you.

Well, for the first time in my life, I was deeply, profoundly, and completely convicted that day. It was in that moment I knew that I had to clean up my life. I won't say how but suffice it to say, it was extensive and deeply humbling as I began to get right with him. In a short time, I removed from my apartment everything that would displease him, and I vowed that I would never fail him in that way again.

But also, I knew it was time to seek him and put myself in his hands. He had orchestrated all this, and there was no way out for me. I knew that until I learned the lessons he wanted me to learn, it would not end. Looking back, they were such hard lessons, but honestly, I was so disobedient, strong willed, and independent, it took his extraordinary measures to break me and to get me right with him. I needed his boot camp.

So, as I sat day after day in total isolation, I began to earnestly and humbly journal, pray, and read my Bible. I had no distractions anymore because I had no contact with the outside world, except church on Sunday, and the internet chat lines.

Then one night, in March 2007, after being on my knees in prayer for a very long time, he dictated a letter to me. I remember thinking at the time if what I wrote would make sense after I wrote it all down or would it be gibberish. Well, to my surprise it did make sense.

Below are his dictated words to me that evening. It was the beginning of my new life in him, and the day I truly began to surrender to him. You might think this letter sounds harsh in places, but I consider it a beautiful and caring love letter. It was screaming 'in your face' top kick sergeant boot camp talk, but I needed it.

Part of it also was him helping me begin to take him seriously and fear him. As it says in Isaiah 33:6 NIV:

"In that day he will be your sure foundation, providing a rich store of salvation, wisdom, and knowledge. The fear of the Lord will be the key to this treasure."

Here's what he wrote me, unedited.

"It's not about food, it's not about money it's about me. Put down your will Laura. Do you want to see your calling in me? Then be in me. I have given you the opportunity to get into me. Are you ready to live day by day, without a future? Are you ready to give up control? Are you ready to die every day? Are you willing to give everything away? Are you willing to accept who I need you to be? Are you done planning? Are you done thinking? Are you done strategizing? Are you done being in charge? Will you give me full unending total control of your life? Are you ready to make humility who you are? Are you ready to devote every waking hour to my truth in the word? Are you ready to trust me to take you into dangerous areas? Are you ready to accept me?

I want you to study the Scripture fully; all the time. Write and journal and discover yourself in me. We have 11 years to make up for, will you do the work I need you to do? Even if they throw you in jail? Even if you are to die, will you do my will in all things? It's time to shut up and learn. Do not speak, listen and be of good insight. Know my words. Stand now and wait for me to come for you. Ready yourself to go where I call you to go. Be ready to jump. Be ready to jump. Stay with me Laura, stay here and do this work or I will say to you, 'I never knew you'. This is a work you must complete. The time is short, and you have wasted far too much time already. Listen for me when I knock. Ready the door. Let us dine together. Let me truly be your best friend. Let the truth be known to you. Set your mind free and embrace new vistas, new beginnings; all things new. Get very secure in me, be humble and be ready to move. Listen wait and learn. There's a season your seeds went in, let us work together on your heart. Come back to the table with an attitude of readiness and humility and a closed mouth and an open heart to receive and learn. Live me, breathe me; be me, Laura. No more games. The battle is at hand, and you are not ready. You are not equipped. You do not even know where the battle lies. You are just a baby again, hunny. Embrace your future as my daughter, not as Laura. Feel me, it's not over. Listen and be still. You are not of this earth. Stop being in it. Be my daughter in me.

Do not worry, have I not provided a storehouse for you. Now go with strength in the knowledge that as long as I know the plan, you do not need to. Study me, become me until I tell you different. Remove from your life absolutely anything that does not directly glorify me in some way. From brownies to not exercising, stop playing at life, it's time to get to work. Your call Laura but remember, I am watching. Please, Laura, don't be burned alive for all eternity, come to me, will you?

YES NO   x_____ "

I sat there on the floor looking at my journal, re-reading this letter, and pondering much.

The first part was all about my willingness. Then there was this line, "Now go with strength in the knowledge that as long as I know the plan, you do not need to." Talk about faith and trust!

"Are you willing to have me take you into dangerous areas?" At the time I thought he meant mission trips to Africa or something but I've come to understand over the years that what he meant was taking me into situations and circumstances that required me to seek him for faith, and the courage in him to walk through it, like writing this book.

But what I looked at the most was that line with the 'x.'

I knew that writing 'yes' was meaningless without it being sincere. I was a veteran Christian enough to know the seriousness of what he was asking. He was making it clear to me, "I never knew you." Right out of Matthew 7:23 He also made it very clear what my fate was, at the end of what he said to me if I said 'no.'

The Bible speaks about a lukewarm church in revelation, and I knew he was calling me out as a lukewarm believer, ready to spit me out of his mouth. I had to start taking my walk seriously. I had to begin to fear him and obey him without question. To sign that line 'yes' would require me to be 'all in', holding nothing back.

I did sign that line 'yes', but it was after much prayer and personal soul searching because I knew he would demand obedience, willingness, and commitment in my walk that I had never given him before. It meant that there was no turning back and that whatever he said to me would need to be humbly followed and obeyed.

It was the beginning of my training in knowing his voice and learning to be the daughter and sister in the Lord for others he wanted me to be.

Funny, that in this time of personal self-discovery, he was also showing me who I was in him as his daughter.

Chapter 13

"All Scripture is inspired by God and is useful to teach us what is true and to make us realize what is wrong in our lives. It corrects us when we are wrong and teaches us to do what is right." 2 Timothy 3:16 NLT

THIS WAS an incredible time for me, yet it would appear to an outsider that God was being harsh with me. But honestly, it was the most loving thing he could do for me. I had become very stubborn, independent, and unwilling to follow. But in this time he was showing me I was to follow him. This was tough love. I didn't see it that way at the time. In many ways, I was suffering terribly, yet as the saying goes, "I wouldn't buy the experience for a nickel, but I wouldn't sell it for a million dollars."

I was journaling for hours daily, and I read most of the Bible. He even had me read the entire book of Isaiah and Jeremiah out loud. That's actually an amazing thing to do because the words come alive in a whole new way when you read them out loud.

In this time, he also showed me how to hear and know his voice. He shared with me rules about knowing for sure it was him, and rules about sharing the words I would get for others.

He gave me a ministry to go on chat lines, and he led me to encourage women in desperate need of his love anywhere in North America.

Over those few months, I called over fifty women, including three women on a single Friday night talking about ending their life.

Much of the time he would just impart a verse for me to share.

The thing I grew to understand, that is still the case today, is that the words he gives me for others are never new to the recipient. They are simply to impart a truth they already know or challenge them to start something he was bugging them to start or stop something he was bugging them to stop.

Here are several stories of his training me up in this time.

Chapter 14

THERE WAS an entire morning he had me read and ponder Romans 1:1 *"Paul, a servant of Christ Jesus, called to be an apostle and set apart for the gospel of God."* (NIV)

This was an awesome exercise because I deeply pondered what it was to be a servant. What did that truly mean for Paul? What does that mean for you and for me?

Then he wrote, 'Set apart.' What does that mean? Are we all set apart? What does that look like in our lives if we are?

You can answer those question quickly and keep reading, or you can put this book down for a time and give yourself time to ponder this verse and seek him as I did.

Know, however, that it was the three hours of re-reading this verse that made the experience worthwhile. Even just re-reading it, and putting emphasis on different words ultimately helped me deepen my understanding and commitment to him.

There was an afternoon that I tossed my Bible across the room and onto the couch. I did that quite often, but that day it didn't go over well. He told me that from now on I was to read the Bible on my knees. So I asked him what to read. He said Psalm 4. I read it, and then asked him what now? He said Psalm 4. Ha, yeah, I got the hint. I just kept reading Psalm 4 over and over.

Funny thing was that after about an hour of this, I found myself sinking lower and lower, and the Bible was getting higher and higher. So I prayed and asked him if I had to keep doing this.

He told me, 'no,' but that it was about time I begin to cherish that book. That he was in there; his heart and his will for us, he himself was in that book, and I needed to treat it with the respect it was due. It wasn't really about the Bible though; it was about respecting him.

Years later I caught my roommate Sarah tossing her Bible, and I freaked on her. I picked it up, kissed it, and gently handed it back to her, then I shared with her what I learned that day.

There was the day I got my welfare check, and I needed to go to a cheap supermarket to finally get some food. However, there was a catch.

I needed to take the bus south for a few minutes, and then transfer and go east. That was perfectly acceptable to get a transfer from the driver going south, and then flash the transfer to the driver going east when I got on the second bus. Unfortunately, after I got off the first bus, I had to walk two blocks to the bank to cash my welfare check. But by doing so, the rules state that if you leave the transfer area, i.e. the corner, you must pay another two dollars and not use the transfer.

God made that very clear to me before I got on the first bus that I couldn't use a transfer and not to take one from the driver. Yet, two dollars was a lot of money to me! So, when I got on the first bus, I ignored God and took a transfer. When I got off the bus at the transfer location, I walked the two blocks, cashed my check, and returned. Again, God was all over me to pay again and not use that transfer. Yet, when the bus came, I used the transfer and didn't pay.

As I got off the bus at my destination, he stopped me in the parking lot and slammed me to my knees. He was so angry with me. He DEMANDED that I double pay when I reboarded the bus to go home. This wasn't a request, and he made it clear that he was done with me if I defied him again.

At the time, I didn't honestly see what the big deal was. It was only two dollars, and I was only at the bank for five minutes. No one saw, knew or cared including me, and the bus driver I wager. Yet, I knew God was serious and meant it by how harshly and profoundly he humbled me.

So after shopping, I stood at the bus stop with a double payment to put in the box. I had six dollars left for the rest of the month, and I imagined perhaps getting a few vegetables later in the month with the money, but I knew that I had to use four of it right then.

As the bus came and began to cross the street to the stop, he gently said to me, "Don't double pay; only pay the two dollars."

I was nearly in tears because at that point my sin began to sink in.

I had the heart of a thief!

When I got home, I sought him immediately. I was so sorry and so humbled. I knew I had failed him and that he was so displeased with me. I knew he loved me and that I had let him down. I felt so sad and so sick.

He gently said to me that it wasn't about the money but about my heart and my character. He told me, 'if I couldn't be trusted with two dollars, how could I be trusted with $200,000 dollars that I would handle later in my life?' My heart wasn't pure, and my motives were sinful. To him, that two dollars was as important for me to honour as two million. Stealing is stealing; regardless of the amount and he would not stand for it from me any longer.

I've never handled $200,000, but I know in my deepest heart that I would honour him and could now be trusted with it. It was just two dollars but ultimately for me that day, it also became as important as two million. I never let him down again in this. Stealing starts in the heart and mine still needed much work. I was so desperate to change, and I sought to stop stealing and to be an honest person for the first time in my life!

"Whoever can be trusted with very little can also be trusted with much, and whoever is dishonest with very little will also be dishonest with much. So if you have not been trustworthy in handling worldly wealth, who will trust you with true riches?" Luke 16:10-11 NIV

About five weeks later, a check-out clerk gave me change for twenty dollars when I only handed her a ten dollar bill. There was no consideration or hesitation from me at all, I told her that she gave me too much change, but she wouldn't listen. Four more times I pleaded with her that she gave me too much change.

Unfortunately, she still wouldn't listen even though I kept trying to tell her she overpaid me. She kept thinking I was telling her that she owed me, and she kept insisting that she gave me the correct change. Sadly, she never considered that I could be helping her out by finally doing the right thing. Eventually, I kept the money and walked out when it was clear that she would not take it back from me.

I was so pleased and thankful to God for my changed heart. I wanted to be trustworthy, and I wanted others to know I could be trusted. I wanted God to be proud of me. What surprised me was that my reaction was immediate and instant, I never thought about keeping it. That money wasn't mine, and I needed to give it back.

About two years ago, I bought a bunch of things at IKEA that were on a flat cart as I went through the self-checkout. As I loaded the items in my car, I saw an item that was lying flat that I never paid for. I finished loaded my car, then without hesitation, I grabbed the unpaid item and marched back into the store to pay for it.

I approached the cashier in charge of self-check-out and told her that I found an item on my cart that I never paid for and that I wanted to pay for it. She was absolutely stumped as she responded, "But you were out of the store already, why did you come back?"

I looked at her, and I said from my heart, "I'm a Christian, and I want to honour God in my life, and I don't steal."

She shook her head in disbelief as she took my money.

When I got to the car, I began praising God. I never thought for even a split second about keeping that item without paying for it. I was so thankful that I brought honour to his name by my changed heart. On top of that, I showed someone what doing the right thing looked like. It was an opportunity to say I follow Jesus and I have been set apart as a result. (Romans 1:1)

Now, my heart and my life - my entire being, is to follow Jesus. I have a desperate yearning desire to forever press on to that goal, in every area of my life and to be like him in every way. And it all began with two dollars and a new-found willingness to let him change me.

It was in this time that he gave me this saying.

Doing the right thing isn't always easy, but it's always right.

I've discovered over the years that doing the right thing is almost never easy, yet, we are called to be set apart and take that item back into the store and pay for it. Having faith and trust to do his will without question is what he calls us to walk out.

God isn't looking for perfect people; he's just looking for willing ones. Willing to let him work on us and trust him to do it. If you're reading this and saying to yourself, wow, she has it all together, what chance do I have? Don't! I need him every day. I was so thankful that the lessons learned about having an honest heart in '07 were still present that day at IKEA, but that was ultimately him in me.

I've learned to be humble and willing to surrender when I seek him. He has always met me and helped me when I approach him in that heart place.

Chapter 15

ONE SUNDAY NIGHT I spoke to a college student that I knew online from Miami. She was highly anointed and deeply in touch with the Lord. She was more in touch with the Holy Spirit than anyone I've ever met to date, and she hadn't even been saved a year. God had chosen her, and truly set her apart and be his voice.

She didn't speak often, but when she did, her words were so deep and insightful. She was born to be a true prophet. I knew his voice well, but she was so close to him that it was like she *was* his voice.

She told me that God instructed her to send me $600 for food and that she would send it to me later in the week. I was overjoyed! $600 could buy me a storehouse of food. At my present consumption, that was over a years' worth! It was huge for me. What a blessing! I could actually eat every day!

However, over the next few days, I found myself beginning to think of ways to spend that money unwisely. Spending it on take-out and pricey restaurants instead of buying lasting and basic healthy food and being smart with it.

By Thursday, on my own and still starving, and without God's prompting in any way, I contacted her and told her I couldn't accept the money. She was stunned because she knew how little food I had. But even more, she was quite insistent that God told her to do this, and she never disobeys him.

I let her know that I wasn't a good steward and that my heart wasn't ready for it. I knew I needed to live on the barley soup (i.e. manna) he was providing me and not accept what would have been akin to dropping a giant 7-Eleven in the middle of the desert then telling the Israelites that they can give up manna and have all the chips and Slurpees they want.

She then said that God had asked her to use her rent money to give to me. On blind faith, she was willing to hand over all her rent money to me! On faith!

I realized that he was testing us both. He was testing her willingness to trust him and give her rent money to me, and he was testing me to see if I knew I wasn't ready to receive it. It was the most beautiful thing to be part of, and I am so thankful that I chose the right path.

So often because of difficult circumstances, we can sin in order to alleviate the tough times we face. But God's in those tough times! He allows them, and he will see us through them. When we sin to circumvent them, you and I know that it's not his will for us. But also, I needed the tough times; it's what was changing me for the better.

However, let me be clear, I'm not for a moment suggesting you hand away your savings or something. She knew his voice exceptionally well and is the most anointed person I've ever encountered in my life. The enemy can whisper in our ears too. The reason why she got upset when I told her I couldn't accept the money was because she was 100% certain that he told her to do it, and she was desperate as I was, not to let him down.

Being willing isn't something you do; it's a state of mind and a readiness to serve him as he directs.

I don't tout anything I did in this. It was God helping me discover the true nature of my heart as he worked to rid me of so much sin in my life. My heart was changing but how can it not change when you're being mentored by the Holy Spirit himself?

Chapter 16

The amount God will be able to use you is in direct proportion to the amount of humility you have.

THERE WAS a major issue about myself that God needed me to understand and overcome. He told me to leave the church in my old neighborhood which I had been attending for the past year. I obeyed and let the pastors know.

Let's just say that I got a very unpleasant response from them. They said that God would never tell anyone to leave the church and that I was just lazy about finding work, and that God would not honour my actions and I deserved all the hardship I got. They quoted Scripture to back up their assertion, and yet, in the end, they simply showed me what they really thought of me.

Well, I prayed about it more and asked the Lord why he had me leave. His answer was direct, and life altering in its bluntness. "I'm saving them from you."

He then went on to tell me that I have always walked into a church with a heart that said, "What can I get? What can I take?" He said that I would not enter a church again until I had a heart that asked, "What can I give? How can I serve?"

I did attend another church on occasion after that, yet I didn't go in looking to get from them. But to be honest, it wasn't until the summer of 2016, and coming to the church I now attend, that I truly gained a genuine heart to give and serve and no desire to take.

Could I receive from others? Yes, absolutely, if they choose to give to me, but I don't take from them.

He also said that my priority for my entire life has always been: "Laura, Laura, Laura." He then said that from now on it needs to be, "God, Others, Laura."

"Jesus replied: "'Love the Lord your God with all your heart and with all your soul and with all your mind.' This is the first and greatest commandment. And the second is like it: 'Love your neighbor as yourself.'" Matthew 22:37-39NIV

I have to ask you, where's your heart and attitude when you enter a church? Do you roll in late every week? (That's a huge red flag!) Do you never get involved but enjoy the church experience at the expense of others and then leave having checked church off your list of things you needed to accomplish? Are you one of the 90% statistically who regularly attend church, who take and never give or get involved? I'm not speaking about one-offs or unavoidable commitments, but a habitual pattern you purpose to walk out.

Speaking as someone who knows, 'God, others, me' can only come when you have a heart that seeks to give and not take.

Is your priority, 'God, others, me?'

It can be if it's not. If we seek him in humility and a willingness to change, I can tell you that it can.

Something to ponder and seek our Lord about.

Chapter 17

THE LAST STORY I want to share with you is the day I was downtown at an appointment. I had arrived by streetcar and was standing in a crowd of about twenty people waiting for the next streetcar to take me home. I looked around and saw an entrance to an underground grocery store. So with my last sixty-five cents, I went downstairs and purchased an apple, then came back up to stand with the others while holding the apple.

It had been five months since I had fresh fruit, yet I couldn't bear to bite into it because it smelled so good. I knew that if I bit into it, in a very short time it would be gone and I wanted to savor it all I could. I just kept smelling it, when out of the blue God spoke to me and said, "Do you have any idea how many apples you let go rotten in the bottom of your fridge?"

I was so convicted in that moment, and I felt such immediate shame because I know how many full bags of apples went to the trash over the years. Then moments later he continued, "Do you have any idea how many apples you only took one bite out of and then threw away?"

At this point, the tears began to stream down my face as I was even more convicted. Then he said, "Have you EVER ONCE considered or appreciated who provided you with all the meals you've eaten in your life?"

I was so overwhelmed! I was barely holding on because he was right! He was so right! God is worthy of so much more from me. Jesus came and died so I might have life. The greatest gift was himself. He saved me from killing myself that day, then two years later he led me home to himself. Yet, I had never appreciated my salvation or the food he provided. I had not appreciated anything he ever gave me! I now knew more of my massive sin against him.

He was showing me that the best part of my salvation is my relationship with Jesus and the shared adoration between my loving Saviour and myself.

Yet, I knew that I needed to do a lot better, not because he demanded it but because I had it within me to do so and he deserved it. I wanted to do better, and I was going to do better. I was desperately seeking to get right with him, and I would not stop until I truly appreciated him in both my heart and my life.

Still standing on the street, I prayed and told him that I didn't want the apple anymore. He then told me to eat it but remember in every bite how thankful I need to be, and who deserves the thanks.

I quietly wept tears of shame, guilt and thankfulness as well, as I sat on the streetcar eating my apple slowly, and praying with every bite.

Since that day I've never taken the food, he's given me for granted. For anything, he's given me really. I became so much more thankful after that day. I know I'm not perfect, and I don't always get things right, but I'm still desperate to be thankful. Even in the small things, I seek to thank him.

My friends often wonder why I'm forever telling them why I'm so thankful for them - because I am! I am so blessed by God with very kind and loving people in my life that I deeply cherish as gifts from God. I have come to a place in my life that if I was to go home to him, those in my life would have recently been told how much I love and appreciate them.

That day marked the largest shift in my heart in this time. I hadn't arrived, but he set my heart on the right path that day. He was making me honest, humble, and thankful and I was desperate to walk it out.

These were just some of the many things he showed me in this time.

He told me in April that I was going to be moving and not in the Toronto area.

Six weeks later he told me to put my resume out to one company in the US, and in just a few days I was hired by them on the spot and handed $4000 cash to move. Instantly I went from $625 a month to $4000 a month. Despite those pastors telling me I was a loaf and quoting Scripture that said so, I knew in my heart that until I had received what he wanted me to learn, God wasn't going to allow me a job.

So what can I say about God's boot camp?

I became serious about my walk, willing, humble and committed to doing his will. He showed me a better way to live, and a profound desire to following him.

He didn't allow me to get away with anything and was very hard on me for the smallest things. It really was boot camp. He helped me get rid of many sinful issues and habits, and he helped me begin to see my future in him. Above all, he taught me to walk in holiness and humility, and at a minimum, he showed me the path I needed to be on to walk those out.

As with any soldier, boot camp is just the beginning of creating an experienced, skilled, and valuable soldier. I had gone through his boot camp, and it was now time for me to begin to truly be a disciple of Christ instead of the slouch I was before.

Most of all, it helped me rely on him alone. He toughened me up and helped me gain a deeper connection with him by knowing his voice so I would seek him in every circumstance. It's kind of like that saying, 'you ask ten people a strictly 'yes' or 'no' question, somehow you end up with ten different answers.' You ask God the question, and you get one right answer every time. He was helping me seek him out first, and not last like we are all prone to do in our life.

I was excited to have my new heart, and I was so thankful to him for a second chance. I was so fast to listen, and do as he showed me.

I was his, and I finally appreciated his love for me.

Chapter 18

My Church Life

TWO YEARS earlier in 2005, at the time I was in the middle of self-discovery, I began electrolysis with a woman who was a Christian. This was an interesting relationship we developed over the dozens of hours we spent together. I would play John McArthur, Alastair Begg, and James MacDonald preaching recordings, among others, to pass the time. I enjoyed the teaching and yet hearing through her niece, I knew this perplexed her. How could I, a transgendered (or so I thought I was at the time) confused soul be saved and listening to radio preachers? As far as she was concerned my deviant lifestyle while claiming to be saved were at odds, and yet she knew I was a Christian.

She had seen a few transgendered clients over the years, but they weren't saved, so she pegged them as unsaved heathens who didn't understand the gravity of the sin they were doing but I was different, I was saved, and it bothered her black and white understanding.

At one point, she asked me if I would be interested in attending her home group since I hadn't connected with a new church yet. I agreed, and I went to her small group, and ultimately began to attend the church as well. What I came to discover later by her own admission was that before I attended the small group, she told them that I wasn't a woman.

The small group leader, also by her own admission, had broken the confidence of our group by going to the pastors quietly to let them know about me.

I first began to suspect something was wrong when two months later I was at a mission function on a Saturday morning at the church. Another woman from my table and I were getting something at the buffet when the senior pastor of our church came up beside me. I had never met him before, but when he turned and saw me standing there, he gave me this look. My companion described the look perfectly. After he left she asked me, "Wow, what did you do to him, kill one of his kids?"

I turned to her still stunned and said, "I've never met him before."

"Well, you must have done something?" She responded.

I stayed at that church for a short time, but I ultimately left.

At this point, I was growing in my understanding of who I was, but also all that was done to me in my past was now surfacing in my conscious mind. The pain and abuse I had endured all started to come back to me. In turn, I began a desperate search for caring people to help me work through it. I was in deep need of people to love me. I didn't need counselling; I needed a caring community, based in love to help me overcome this.

I was alone and was in a bad way emotionally. My outward persona was falling apart, and I tried to appear okay, but I wasn't. I had a volcano sized amount of pain, hurt, anger, and bitterness all stemming from this massive injustice done to me and it was beginning to boil up out of me. I needed to channel it safely and work through it. It was a jumble of bitter emotions, and like an unstoppable train, it was coming.

Chapter 19

My first brush with a fear monger

"Dear children, let's not merely say that we love each other; let us show the truth by our actions. Our actions will show that we belong to the truth." 1 John 3:18-19a NLT

A YEAR BEFORE God's boot camp, I began attending a church downtown. I kept my past to myself, and in some ways, I had made some great strides in fitting in and learning to let go and just be myself. Yet, ultimately, I really wasn't. I had to hide my past to be accepted, but more than that, I couldn't seek the desperately needed support and comfort from the other women in the church that I needed. Eventually, out of desperation, I approached a few of them independently and shared my story.

They were all leery, and somewhat taken aback, not exactly knowing what to do or say. Yet, they all asked me the same question, had I told Linda yet. They each independently agreed that if there was one person who would understand me, and help me overcome much, it would be Linda. She was unanimously voted the most loving and caring woman in the church.

I had already spent a lot of time with Linda. We had done the girlfriend lunch more than once, and I had sat in her backyard on more than one occasion. I appreciated her and we were becoming really good friends.

So one afternoon I sat with her with the intention to tell her. She said the same sentence everyone says to me before I share my story, "Oh Laura, no matter what you tell me, I'll still love you. Nothing you say could possibly change my love for you."

So, I told her my story in the hope that with her assurance of love and the assurances of so many others, she could help me overcome so much pain I was suffering through alone.

Sadly, however, in less than twenty-four hours she began a campaign to lynch me and became one of the greatest fear mongers I have ever encountered in my life.

She started telling everyone some twisted fear-based gossip about me, and suddenly, so many people who knew me well were keeping their distance from me. A few days later at an outdoor event at the church, I saw her going from person to person, talking to them and pointing at me and then watching the person gain a fearful expression. One woman, I knew well actually ran and grabbed her kids into herself as she stared at me gasping.

At one point that day, I had the opportunity to hold a newborn in my arms as he slept so peacefully. Such a joyful experience! I just stared at him and touched his tiny little fingers and kissed him so many times; he was truly a gift from God. I don't have the opportunity to hold babies often, but when I do, I enjoy it so very much. Eventually, I gave him back and moved away. I turned back a moment later to see Linda pounce on the mother of the newborn, pointing at me and frantically telling her that a monster had held her newborn or some such thing. Yet, the mom just continued to looked at me with gentle eyes. Perhaps it was because she watched me with her son and knew better? Or perhaps something deeper? I knew her, and she had a gentleness and a deep peace about her. Perhaps she was looking at me through the loving eyes of Christ, and not the eyes of fearful Linda?

Sadly, in the end, I witnessed that day my closest friend at the church, who pledged to love me 'no matter what', try her best to ruin me with gossip and have me run out of her church on a rail in a matter of only a few days.

A week later, I approached the assistant pastor for help as the senior pastor was on vacation. She told me that she would speak to Linda and have her stop the witch hunt, fear mongering, and gossip. However, she said that by law, (not sure what law that is!) she was now obligated to inform the elders, deacons, side persons and all their spouses; most of the church in the end, that "There's a man in our church pretending to be a woman." Her words! Despite my best effort to share my story with her, that was her takeaway.

It was so disheartening to me because only a week earlier I was well liked, and for the first time in my life I was myself and felt like I belonged somewhere. Then a week later after my meeting with the associate pastor, I came to church, and I began to sit down in one of the pews. Instantly, everyone left the pew I sat in. Then they left the surrounding pews as well. I had three full pews to myself as people crammed themselves into the remaining ones to physically avoid me.

Except for one twenty-two-year-old woman I was friends with. She didn't know about me because she'd been away; Linda hadn't spread her lies to her yet. This young woman sat down beside me, and I immediately saw those around us trying to get her attention to warn her to move away from me. I saw such hate in their eyes. Yet, she saw I was emotionally distraught and stayed with me. She must have wondered why everyone was nearly sitting on each other in the other pews while leaving three pews totally empty.

She kept asking me what was wrong as my tears increased near the end of the service. I collapsed into her lap sobbing uncontrollably. She didn't know what to do to try to console me. In time I sat up and told her that I was hated by everyone, and I was a leper, and that she will hate me too when she hears. Well, guess what she said in response? "Oh,

Laura, there's nothing I could learn about you that would stop me from loving you."

Well, on my own, a few days later we met in private, and I told her. I wanted it to come from me so it would be the truth and not Linda's twisted gossip. Eventually, she backed away from me as well. She was young, and I suspect she sought counsel from one of the lynch mob.

The next Sunday I came to church and began to enter the church lobby when Linda and her husband stopped me. They told me that since they considered me a man, they would now use my male name given to me at birth and let everyone know what it is and demand that they all use it. She then proudly spoke it out loud. Her husband was a former police officer, so I suspect they illegally ran me through the system to find out my old name as I have never shared that name with anyone. Today, not even my closest friends know it. That name I was given at birth represents all the torture I endured. I cringe even now when I hear it because it still provokes agonizing memories.

For Linda to use it was the biggest betrayal of all. If she disagreed with me, that's one thing. If she felt the need to make me out to be a monster and encourage everyone to lynch me, who am I to stop her. But when she used that name she crossed the line! She took a lifetime of pain, misery, uncertainty, fear and heartache rolled up into one name then slapped me hard across the face with it. Even now, there's nothing more hurtful a person could do to me than to purposely call me by that name.

In my entire life to date, I have never felt more betrayed. Appreciate that statement later when you read further into this book. This betrayal was orchestrated by a woman who thirty seconds before I told her was one of the most 'loving Christians' I ever knew.

So, back in the lobby not skipping a beat, she then said to me with a profoundly haughty and righteous tone that I was an abomination to the Lord and I needed to repent, casting her judgment upon me from on high.

In that moment, fear and dread welled up in me as I stared at Linda's snotty, smug face and haughty eyes, as she grinned at me in victory. I knew I would once again feel the sting of isolation and loneliness as I turned and left.

I had made so many good friends, and I felt like I had found a family there, it was hard to let that all go! Every week after the Sunday night service, a group of us would go to the local pub and enjoy the evening before heading home. We'd have a pint and some pub grub and good times. It was such a good time for me, and I enjoyed it so much. I was finally interacting with others as the real me, and I was learning so much about myself. They were a great group of people, and I fit in and was deeply appreciated. When I turned and left the church, in that moment I knew that was to end as well.

Why are people so ready and willing to believe something negative about a person without even giving them the benefit of the doubt? Yet, we find it hard to believe a positive thing said about another.

"At such moments, we need courage to stand up to hate, not just in others but in ourselves." Barack Obama

I ended up in a deserted park sobbing and wailing to God. I just wanted to be loved for who I was. Was it so much to ask that people could love me and stop there? I wasn't a bad person I was just desperate to be part of a family. I was desperate for acceptance, affection and to heal from the pain of my past.

A few weeks later, the senior pastor very politely asked me if I would be willing to meet him in private. When we met, he told me that I was a fool to say anything and that there was a woman in the congregation who had the full gender reassignment surgery eight years previous. He stated that she saw what they were doing to me but couldn't help me because she feared that Linda might find out about her.

How sad is that!

He told me that if I am the woman I know myself to be, I need to shut up about my past and just be the woman God made me to be. Laughingly at the time, I thought about contacting Linda to tell her that there was a 'man' in the church who had the surgery to become a woman and then watch Linda go looney for weeks trying to find the boogeyman under every skirt. But I knew she was relentless and that I could never be part of the lynching of an innocent person.

I took his advice, and after that, I kept my past to myself but looking back it was the worst advice imaginable! It kept me from seeking help because it prevented me from being authentic. I had to hide behind a persona again because I had to invent a past and lie to make myself acceptable. Ultimately I was trapped again because I couldn't be entirely authentic.

Basically, this man told me to lie and keep the truth about my secret and not deal with my unresolved pain. So in future when people got to know me, they learned to like a lie because I couldn't tell them everything about myself and seek people out who would love me regardless of my past.

I was living in the shadows again and appeasing others at my own expense like I had all my life. But what choice did I have? I had to suffer with my emotional past rising up within me in silence. The alternative was to be abused all over again; just by different people.

I spent several months out of church entirely because I was still reeling from the hurt Linda had caused. I felt so alone and so trapped, and it seemed that no matter what I did someone was ready to stone me.

Eventually, I began attending a church near my home, and I kept my story to myself the entire time I was there. I stayed there all through God's boot camp time until God told me to leave.

Today as I wrote what happened at this church I began to cry. I had done nothing wrong! I was only trying to cope with an impossible situation. I didn't understand all of what was going on with me, I just knew that I did nothing to deserve what was being perpetrated against me. All I wanted was to belong for the first time in my life. I went there to find the love of Jesus and yet what I found instead was fear motivated bigotry and hatred.

Seeing Linda turn on me as she did still haunts me as I discovered today in tears. No one ever did such an about-face when I told them. I openly and genuinely loved her. My walls were down with her, and this is what she did in return when I chose to trust her. There's already such pain, violence, bigotry and hatred in our world. Why must we Christians add to it?

Could there ever be a time when we could simply love everyone no matter what? Where someone could show us a better way to treat each other? Where love would be our ONLY response to each other; regardless of what we hear or see? Actually, there was a time when that happened. It was 30AD, and his name was Jesus.

Sadly, Linda professed to follow him while she sought to destroy me.

I thought I was over all that happened to me by her hand. I thought I was through the pain, and then as I wrote this chapter today, I remembered many things; like the space they gave me in the pews, and my tears began. It just struck me so hard because they didn't care that they were hurting me.

When I got home that day after church, being so isolated in the pews, I wrote about my experience over those few weeks. I want to share it with you because I think it lets you in on where I was in my journey at the time. It's one thing to write this book, so many years later but it's entirely different to share a piece I wrote at the time it was happening.

Our actions towards others have consequences! I'm including this piece here to help us all remember the pain we can cause others when we walk in anger, fear and self-righteousness towards them. It's very real and very damaging and not what Jesus showed us to do at all!

To be alone in a church full of people

To be hated by some, rejected by some, tolerated by some, loathed by some and marginally accepted by some is the hardest thing one can ever face in one's life. To be completely alone and isolated in a church full of people, is so sad and so defeating. To be loved and cared about by everyone at the beginning, and then to have it ripped away to be replaced with isolation, bigotry and profound loneliness leads one to a place of deep despair.

A church full of people, loving and caring about each other except for you. To be isolated and told by some to leave the church and never return. To be hated and loathed by ones who cared about you in the beginning. To be judged and condemned to a life and walk, not in fellowship and love in the body of believers but to be handed a sentence of loneliness and despair, in a church full of people because of bigotry.

Alone and isolated, what a sentence. Solitary confinement in a lonely pew, isolated and judged alone and set apart, judged guilty of being different. Set apart and hated from those who once loved you. Trapped in your love of God and your love of others. To be isolated and not allowed to show others the love you have. To be so desperate to know fellowship again as it once was but feeling hatred instead.

Then you begin to fear even coming to church at all. Bigotry rears its ugly head. To be alone in your home, or alone in a church full of people; what's the difference? To be loved and accepted by God but cursed by people who once accepted and loved you.

God loves and commands all to love thy neighbor as thyself. Yet, you take it to heart only to have others ignore it when it comes to you. To feel cold stares, and to experience angry expressions from those who hugged you with love and acceptance in the beginning. Alone in a fishbowl to only bang up against the glass. To see others in deep fellowship; the same kind you once had. But now you sit behind the glass and remember the love in a hug, and the joy of fellowship with so many who now stay away from you. Shunned and hated for being different. Condemned to a life of misery no matter what you do. Live a life of misery, and be accepted by the ones who hate you now, or live as you know you must, yet then live a life of misery because you choose a different path that is not acceptable to them. It is to God but not to them.

To beg on your knees for love and hear silence. To beg for a smile to be met with hate. To wish for fellowship with so many, and to come to a place, where wishes die and despair sets in. To live a life of wandering, looking for a scrap of kindness that the dogs get but instead, feel the pain of isolation. You see someone looking at you with that loving smile, only to realize as they rush past you to hug the person behind you, that you are indeed alone in a church full of people. To wonder what it's like to be loved. To wonder what it's like to be a part of a community. To wonder if God can actually deliver you from being an outcast to being loved by all. Apparently, God has his limits to change minds and people's opinions. You have your loneliness, and others have their self-righteousness, bigotry, and hate.

To be alone in a church full of people.

Today, I thank God that if I was to encounter Linda in my future, I couldn't help but give her a genuine, warm and loving hug.

Believe me, it's not me, but our God is a loving God, and I have been changed by him. Today I'm so desperate to follow Jesus and his example! I couldn't do anything but love her because she's only human and makes mistakes like me and because grace for her fills my heart.

This time for me could have been so special. Imagine what God could have done had they believed in me and rallied around me. They could have truly embraced, loved and walked with me. They could have been there to listen and help me work through so much. What a blessing that would have been for them and me.

Like the two religious men in the parable Jesus taught us in Luke 10 who walked on without helping the injured man in the ditch, the Samaritan man showed compassion and love. This church had the opportunity to do the same but chose to walk in hate instead.

If we as Christ followers refuse to freely give God's unconditional love and compassion in our churches to others, then what's the point of being there? What do the unsaved think of us when we brutally and openly attack others in our church?

They could have been blessed by God for taking a very beat-up traveler in the ditch, in need of love and care and help me recover, grow and flourish in a loving community for the first time in my life. Imagine how it could have been so different had they walked like Jesus in love, grace, gentleness and kindness and not fear, hatred and indifference.

It was my first brush with panic-driven fear, and what it can do to us and those around us when we allow it free reign in our hearts.

Fear mongers think they are doing everyone a public service, yet with any action, there are always repercussions. Linda allowed fear to rule her heart, then gossiped about me to rid her church of the person she considered dangerous to her black and white thinking.

Unchecked, fear can propel us to do such evil.

I've heard it said that God isn't fear, and that fear is the absence of faith. So what then would be the proper word for the presence of faith? Peace? Confidence?

The mother of the newborn baby had God's peace about me despite what Linda told her, yet Linda only had fear. I came to witness Linda's genuine unloving fickle heart, without her loving churchy pretense.

In the end, I was the same person. I hadn't changed nor had Linda. She was just showing me her true heart.

Chapter 20

IN THE SUMMER of 2007, a few weeks after God's boot camp ended, I arrived in Boston to begin my new job. A week later Sarah moved in with me.

Sarah was a sweet and kind young woman who I talked to often on the internet. She had moved in with me to go to college locally, as well as save her parents money in dorm costs as she was attending college far away. I had space, and she was a joy to have around. She was from the Boston area, and she knew my story, had seen my body naturally, and was such a fantastic chum. She and I were genuinely close friends, and we enjoyed each other's company. At times I felt like a spiritual mentor, a big sister, and other times I felt more like a second mom.

We began attending a church together, and in time I joined the worship team singing opposite the worship leader while Sarah sang backup. Sarah and I were both very active in the church. Small group was great, and things were going so well for me.

God had, for the most part, stopped using me for the prophetic, unlike my time in boot camp. But I was okay with it because I knew I was a honed and sharpened tool on his work bench, and when he needed me I was there and willing to be used.

He only used me once in the first year I was there, and I think it's a cool story. I sat with Sarah one Sunday at church near the front. As the service ended, they called for anyone seeking prayer to come forward.

This young woman named Mary from our small group went forward, and the elders began to pray over her.

Sarah said to me, "Can we go?"

I responded, "No, we need to stay. I have a word for someone."

"For who?" she asked.

"I don't know."

So we sat waiting on the Lord.

After a time I said to Sarah, "The message is for Mary."

"What's the message?" She asked.

"I don't know."

Then, a minute later, God shared a verse with me to share with Mary. So as I prepared the Bible to read the passage to her when he instructed me to write the Scripture down instead. So now I'm sitting with this sheet of paper in my hand, and I know the recipient, when Sarah says to me, "Well, go give it to her."

"No, not yet, it isn't time."

"What do you mean? She's right there, go give it to her."

"I can't yet. He'll give me a sign."

After about two minutes of more waiting, one of the elders looked up right at me and smiled broadly. I then knew it was the sign. I stood and walked up to them praying over her, and I said that I have a word for her. I opened the paper and read the Scripture to them.

All three turned to look at me in unison, as their eyes bugged out and their mouths opened in astonishment.

I asked them, "What?"

One of the elders said to me, "We just prayed that verse over her ten seconds ago."

I responded, "Well, it would seem that God wants you to receive it," as I handed her the paper, "so much so, that he specifically asked me to write it down and give it to you."

I left them and returned to Sarah and said, "Okay we can go."

After about a year at this church God asked me this question: "Laura, deep down, why are you on worship team? Deep down, you know that you're up there for the status. You're up there for *you*, not me. You like the importance of being up there, but if you're honest with yourself, you know you're not up there for the right reasons."

After a few minutes to search my heart, I agreed. Deep down, I loved the limelight of being up there, and it wasn't all about him. It was then that I knew I needed to resign.

He then said to me, "You are free to join worship team again when your heart's right and when you don't care if you're worshipping me from the back row or on stage. When it's only about me and not about you, then you'll be ready."

I resigned from worship team and continued to seek him to work past this in my life.

In this time we met a great woman at the church. Sarah and I had her over several times, and we were good friends with her. She was a fellow singer on the worship team, and we really enjoyed her company. I was starting to get close to her, so I felt it appropriate to trust her, and to share my story with her.

Her reaction was like nothing I'd ever seen. It was like I handed her a live grenade and she was hysterical as to what to do with it. My story was too much for her to process and she couldn't cope with it. Secretly, she sought out the leadership and shared my story with them. She was frantic to get rid of this grenade of information I had dropped in her lap.

Well, literally overnight, the leadership became cold and indifferent to me and never stopped prodding me to go back to being, 'The man God made me to be.'

They were also feverishly insistent that Sarah move out as I was a perverted man in denial, and it wasn't right for this impressionable young woman to remain with me. They cornered her regularly about it. Eventually, she emphatically told them to leave her alone. They assumed there was some sort of perverted sexual activities going on when in reality we enjoyed a genuine and loving God-honoring friendship.

At one point, the worship team elders had us over to their home to try their hand at it. It was so clear to myself and Sarah, that none of the leadership saw me as saved anymore, and that I was simply sent by the devil to corrupt this young woman. The only thing I remember clearly about this meeting is at one point they questioned my salvation. I responded that the CD in my car that night featured the track "In Christ alone."

He scowled at me and said, "Oh you mean some sort of secular perverted track with the same name." Yeah, he actually said that!

I said, "No, the same song we sing in church, written by Keith Getty and Stuart Townsend. I have Getty's new CD."

Sarah chimed in as well to defend me. She also saw, as I did, that nothing we said would change their hearts. And it all started because of one woman's inability to cope with the grey zone.

The church was going downhill in this time. The pastor had left already, and these same elders were running it and preaching. One Sunday, one of the elders got up for fifty minutes and talked about the Red Sox. It wasn't a sermon in any way but a sports report. No exaggeration, not one word was about Jesus or God or the Bible, just statistics and player hype. It was truly a pep rally.

In six weeks the church went from 200 to 30. When it hit thirty, Sarah and I left.

We were in the area for only a few more months before I took a job in New Orleans. Sarah came with me because the financial crash had hit and jobs were scarce in the North East. She quickly found a job in NOLA and went to school, and I began my new job.

We began attending a church there, and after a year I got close to several very nice people in my small group. One evening in our home, I shared my story with these few trusted friends. Sadly, they too viciously turned on me. Yet, this time, when they sought out someone in leadership to gossip to about me, this person in leadership would not receive it. She shut them down immediately and chastised them for spreading gossip, and said that she would not entertain it. Then, as one of their pastors in the church, she insisted that they stop the gossip.

This amazing woman stood up for what was honoring to God. She didn't stand up for me in any way, make that distinction; she stood up against gossip. The subject of the gossip was immaterial.

I did share my story with this same woman's pastor, and she was so understanding and genuinely loving to me. Never once have I ever seen her walk in anything but love, gentleness and peace. She has God's heart, and over the years we've known each other she has never stopped showing it to me. I sincerely respect and appreciate her in my life.

Because of the abuse, these people were still giving me every time I came to church, in time, Sarah and I moved on to the last church we attended in NOLA, where I met Tracy. I said nothing to anyone about my condition. Later I'll share three memories from my time there.

About eighteen months later I came back to Canada with Sarah who was going to attend school.

At this point, I was very good at hiding the truth, and I had gained many friends at the last church in NOLA who believed my lies regarding my past. Despite my silence, I was a deeply troubled and an angry person with no safe outlet to share and get past the trauma of what I'd suffered.

It seemed that up until then when I truthfully shared my story, Christians immediately, and with exuberance, were happy to add to my pain by attacking me for a decision my parents made when I was an infant. I came to realize that these people only loved "normal" people, not grey zone people like me.

How can someone truly help you if you can't trust anyone enough to share the grey truth about yourself? When you are forced to bury the truth about yourself for acceptance, it's a lie of the enemy! It's a most hollow acceptance in the end because they grow to believe in a lie and not the real you. Sadly, they never gave me any other option.

Chapter 21

"Therefore everyone who hears these words of mine and puts them into practice is like a wise man who built his house on the rock. The rain came down, the streams rose, and the winds blew and beat against that house; yet it did not fall, because it had its foundation on the rock." Matthew 7:24-25NIV

ONE NIGHT IN late 2010 while attending the last church in New Orleans, God gave me my marching orders in who he wanted me to be. While I was reading the scripture passage below, he told me to become these words. To walk all of them out. To make them who I am and to embrace them and become them. He made it clear that no matter what my future held, I was to live these words out and make them my heart. My attitude, words, and actions had to represent these words.

Here is the passage he told me to become:

"Don't just pretend to love others. Really love them. Hate what is wrong. Hold tightly to what is good. Love each other with genuine affection, and take delight in honoring each other. Never be lazy but work hard and serve the Lord enthusiastically. Rejoice in our confident hope. Be patient in trouble, and keep on praying. When God's people are in need, be ready to help them. Always be eager to practice hospitality. Bless those who persecute you. Don't curse them; pray that God will bless them. Be happy with those who are happy, and weep with those who weep. Live in harmony with each other. Don't be too proud to enjoy the company of

ordinary people. And don't think you know it all! Never pay back evil with more evil. Do things in such a way that everyone can see you are honourable. Do all that you can to live in peace with everyone." Romans 12:9-17 NLT

This was the hardest challenge God had ever given me because in the next chapters I was to endure immense pain at the hands of others. The pain I had endured as a child was to pale in comparison to what I was about to endure more than once. No other time in my life have I ever been more emotional demoralized and damaged than this. Not even Linda and those in the U.S. who turned on me rank to what I was to endure.

I'm certain that had I not gone through God's boot camp, and had years of walking out those lessons I learned, growing and deepening my relationship with God, I would not have survived this time. It was only by my solid and unshakable connection to our sure foundation who is Christ that I held on and made it through. I knew his voice, and in this time he was all I had. He was my one and only hope, and he helped me hide those verses in my heart. (Psalm 119:11) Verse 14 being the hardest of all:

"Bless those who persecute you. Don't curse them; pray that God will bless them." NLT

That single verse forced me to walk in meekness, and have a gentle and quiet spirit (1 Peter 3:4) regardless of what was done to me.

By the way, meekness isn't weakness. Meekness is to have the power but choosing not to wield it. Christ walked in meekness more than any other. He could have called on the father to bring down lightning on every Pharisee on the planet, killing them all, yet he didn't. He ultimately asked God to forgive them, because they didn't know what they were doing, as Jesus was about to give up his life on the cross.

God was telling me in these verses that no matter what was to happen, I was to walk them out for the rest of my life, in his humility and meekness! I had been commanded to take the high road, and not fight back in any way that would dishonour God or have me sin in the process.

You are going to read some of what was done to me and wonder how I never retaliated. Yet, I never did. I never once repaid evil with more evil, because God had called me to do this. He was asking me to walk as Christ; in love and gentleness and at many times, in silence as well.

He was asking me to not only curb my actions towards them but to take on his heart and love them despite all that they were doing to me! I was to turn the other cheek. But it wasn't some churchy expression for me. This was real. It was what he expected me to walk out, for real!

I had no idea at the time that he was asking me to return the evil, hate, intolerance, indifference, and libel done to me with his love and grace, and do it in a way that everyone would see that I was honourable.

Even though they were all about to trash those verses, and stomp them to dust with their misguided and deceitful hearts, actions and words, I was ordered by God to be like his son in every way. Ironically, he was asking me to walk out those same verses that they refused to follow themselves!

So easily we can judge others with Bible verses. I certainly could have done that to those who wanted to hurt me, and yet we cannot! Our walk must focus on us, not others! Verses in the Bible are for us to walk out. When we begin to look at verses in the Bible and think of them for others instead of ourselves, we open ourselves up to commit horrible sin against people. It's kind of like hearing a sermon and thinking, 'Wow, Bill needs to hear this.' No, you need to hear it. When we decide to get ourselves right with God, it becomes a full-time job, because we must humbly admit that we have a never-ending mountain of sin to deal with ourselves

– 'that log in our own eye'. (Matthew 7:5) There's no time to judge others.

We must do the right thing, regardless of the actions of others. We must always examine ourselves against Christ, not others, to ensure we are walking in his footsteps. (2 Corinthians 13:5) Our hearts, actions, and words MUST be Christ-like, regardless of the circumstances; there is no half way in this. Yes, we can fall short of that goal in walking those verses out and seek him to help us, but we must continue to try. But as I've always said, "It's easy to be a Christian when everything is going well, who are you when things aren't?" I also heard once, "Character is who you are when no one's around."

Tested by fire (trials) is the only way to prove that God is in you, and it's the only way to refine you.

An interesting thing to know about firing pots in a kiln. In the firing process, they shrink a lot. As the moisture escapes in the firing, they get smaller. Much of our Christian walk can be prideful and puffed up, yet under fire, all that falls away and a smaller, humbler, and wiser person emerges. Also in the firing, the pot goes from easily crumbled clay to being hardened and strengthened by the same fire.

For us, we end up smaller and stronger, more real and with less pretense. We know to look to him far more than we did before.

I cannot say that I didn't want to strike back for what they did to me but with his help, I remained silent, took those thoughts captive, and sought him further to help me work through them.

Had I not been deeply in touch with how desperately I needed him, every day, every hour, I couldn't have begun to walk this out. It was because of my loving relationship with him, and my sincere desire and willingness to serve him that he could help me succeed in this time. I was desperate to do the right thing, despite the anguish and horror they were to put me through. I was going to honour him.

Emotionally, my focus was on them. Spiritually, my focus was on him. The question was, which was going to capture my heart ultimately?

I came to learn that we cannot allow our actions to be led by our emotions. Our actions must be led by the spirit. We must learn to force our emotions to fall in line with what the Holy Spirit is asking us to do and to walk that out no matter how difficult. It's not to put our emotions down or bury them, but it's to say that they cannot rule our heart and actions. Emotions need to be processed but not through sinful actions.

I read once that the cause of anger is the feeling of injustice. I certainly was outraged and justified in that, but I knew I had to process through my emotions but not act on them. Besides my prayer life, I spoke to my only friend Tracy in New Orleans. She listened and prayed so much with me. Perhaps at the end of this section, you may genuinely grasp my appreciation for her, and why I asked her to write the forward. Many times when I was desperate and about ready to give up, she stuck with me and walked beside me through the worst of it, and helped keep my emotions from overrunning me by pointing me to Jesus in my darkest times of despair, isolation, and loneliness. She never offered herself as a solution but helped me find him in the times that I was so lost.

Sadly, at the end of the time that I'm going to share in the next few chapters, it resulted in massive emotional damage that would affect me for many years. There's a saying, 'hurt people, hurt people,' and I must confess that after this time, I hurt many on a scale that I had never imagined. Not intentionally but because of the abuse that was to come. I ended up passing it on. In the end, they tripled my pain and led me to the very edge of despair.

I leave you with this encouraging poem my dear friend wrote many years ago, as we now move forward into the darkest time of my life.

Shaken,
But not shattered
I stand strong
Though I feel so weak
Motionless in your arms
I feel Your strength and love
That's all that keeps me standing
On this shaky ground
                    -Amie Medeiros

Chapter 22

Into That Darkest Valley

"Being small-minded leads to being small-hearted. We shrivel up in our superiority and judgment when we live from our positions of being IN and all those other sinners being OUT. The more I SEE the depths of my own sin, I'm moved with compassion for others because Papa had to reach far...had to reach low...to reach me. May we ever grow in our ability to say, "I don't know," from a truly humble place. How little we all understand the gospel and its beauty." Susie Scarborough

AFTER ARRIVING in Moncton, New Brunswick in 2011, Sarah and I began attending a small, strict but loving church. In a short time, we were welcomed and fully embraced. I was still lying about my past and remained silent about myself because I couldn't trust anyone. I was still furious and upset, and it was really seeping out of me. They all heard my tone and knew that I was struggling with something, but I never shared despite their requests to help me.

In 2012, after many months of being in the church, I had many girlfriends, and I had spent much time with them; I was part of a real church family, and I was thriving in so many ways.

Then Sarah's mom came to visit.

One afternoon, a few days after she had arrived, I got home from work to find my pastors in the driveway waiting for me. Sarah's mom was gone and they told me so was Sarah. My best friend of five years left without a word. My pastors pushed themselves into my apartment uninvited and sat down opposite me.

My mom had passed away two weeks prior, so I was already struggling, and now my best friend was gone as well. I thought they were there to console me and help me get through this new loss. Instead, they told me they knew I was a man and then interrogated me regarding my past and my assumed perverted sexual relationship with Sarah.

It was starting again!!

After three hours of this, I began to scream at them to leave. When they finally left, I fell apart. I was alone with no one to turn to, no one to console me, no one's arms to rest in as I trembled violently and sobbed. My mom was gone and now Sarah too! Add to that, my church pastors, men I had come to admire and highly respect, had offered me no sympathy at all. They simply came over to interrogate me into confessing what they assumed I did, insinuating such vile sin that I hadn't committed with my friend. Not only that, they dragged poor Sarah into it as well!

They knew my mom had just passed, and I was not coping well, yet they chose to abuse me this day.

After the bushwhacking in my apartment, I stayed away from the church for a few weeks, despite their constant insistence that I meet with them again.

I was utterly demoralized, and I felt so alone. Here I was in a foreign city, with no friends, no family, and no church, and the only hug I got was my own, because no one cared about me, as I sobbed so hard that it was hard to breathe. When I finally came back, I had learned that the pastors had informed most everyone that I was a liar and a man pretending to be a woman.

I found how they treated me upon my return was most comical. I know comical is such a strange word to use, but they were being so absurd. These people had known me for a very long time, loved me, and

90

treated me like any other woman in the church. They easily saw and appreciated the woman I am, and recognized those innate qualities in me in every way. Nothing false about me, no lies or misdirection regarding my gender; I was just being my natural female self.

Then suddenly they considered myself the lie, despite doing life with me and knowing me for so long. Yet, the Christians in California saw the woman in me when I was trying not to be myself.

This group now only considered black and white regarding me. Despite the circumstances or my parents, and the genuine and valid reasons behind my decision to correct my gender in my thirties, they could not accept that in their black and white minds. To them, I was simply a sexually perverted and unsaved heathen who changed my gender mid-go like those "trans people".

No man can fake being a woman for the better part of a year, spending so much time with other women as I did. It's not possible! Women speak on levels men don't even know exists. You can't fake that! I spoke and listened on those levels, and as a result, I shared some close bonds with so many women in the church.

I tried to explain to the pastors the mistake my parents made. Yet, they had already found me guilty, and now they were simply going to prove themselves correct by pigeonholing me into the crime they knew I committed so they could justify their actions against me. They became obsessed to get me to confess that I did something with Sarah. But also, they insisted I go from living in freedom and truth as the woman I am, to go back to the lie that my parents had put on me at birth, and in that they demanded I write up a pastor's approved confession, then deliver it to the whole church as a public apology. In it, I had to state that I was really a man and ask for their forgiveness and help in returning me to be, 'The man God made me to be.'

It was devastating for me, and I never complied.

I did go back one last week. The church was travelling up to a parishioner's home for a party, so I went with this couple up to this person's home. It was a very nice day to be honest, until the evening when the two pastors cornered me in a private room. They blocked the door and interrogated me for another three hours without stopping, each taking turns asking me one question after another, all in the hopes of catching me in a lie, and in a sexual-based sin involving Sarah.

What they didn't understand was that I only lied about my past, nothing else. After God's boot camp, I wasn't a sinful person like before. I was deeply seeking him, and walking a very quiet humble life in Romans Chapter 12. Yet, they kept pushing me to admit that Sarah and I were together, but in the end, exasperated and very frustrated, they found nothing to pin on me, because I had done nothing wrong.

I remember at the time they reminded me of the cop shows and the interrogation room. In those shows, the interrogating cops automatically assume guilt until you can prove you're innocent. These two men were set on pinning their sin on me.

I had responded to them in peace and gentleness that God asked me to walk out, and this bothered them greatly. Despite how much they turned up the heat on me, I was calm. I truly believe that they thought I didn't understand their questions, because their question or accusations, which they really were, were so demeaning and vile in nature that no one could remain as calm as I was. Yet, it was God helping me do just that.

Eventually, the evening ended, and another couple drove me home that night. This couple was totally against me and told me that they considered me a confused man and spoke very unkindly to me during the sixty-minute ride home. I finally defended myself by pointing out to them that the Bible tells us, in many places, to love our brothers and sisters in Christ.

I will never forget her response to me. She said, "Well, we don't have to do that because we don't consider you saved."

Every time I think of that sentence I burst out laughing. It was the most self-serving nonsense ever spoken. They got out of loving me because they deemed me unsaved. How convenient! But Jesus said:

"But to you who are willing to listen, I say, love your enemies!" Luke 6:27aNLT

I'm not sure where I fell between, Christian sibling and enemy to them but it was clear that they were charged by God to love me regardless. They dropped me off that night and cursed me in their hearts. It would be the last time I would attend that church again.

Sadly, this church walked this saying out perfectly:

The only real and lasting divide between people is the one we are pridefully unwilling to cross.

As Tracy said to me so many times during this period, "They will answer to God one day for what they did to you."

At this point, I was done with 'loving Christians' for good. My trust in them was destroyed, along with my trust and belief in the position of pastor. I needed time to recover and heal, yet now my healing not only included my past and what my parents did, I had their betrayal as well. Once again, I was alone and so very hurt. Sarah was gone, my mom was dead, and I was in such a bad way and barely holding on.

Chapter 23

DURING THIS TIME away from church, God finally convicted me of lying about my past. He told me that I had to stop and that in future, for people who would go beyond acquaintance, I needed to share with them my full story. No more lies. If they were to love and accept me, it would be based on the whole truth.

Secondly, he told me that my life was to be an open book and that I was to be very open and transparent with others regarding my faith walk and challenges I faced. I was to be put on display so others could learn from my mistakes and be encouraged by my successes, this book being the pinnacle of that command.

Lastly, he told me to go to every person I had lied to that I still had contact with, and confess to them that I had been lying to them. Seek their forgiveness, and then share with them, the truth about myself.

I don't suspect I could have done it had I not gone through God's boot camp. But I wasn't alone in this commandment. Zacchaeus, the tax collector in Luke 19, also had to make things right and not just stop his sin.

I was being asked to do the same. But more than that, I needed to walk out those verses in Romans, and I knew that honourable people speak the truth at all times.

Here is the standard of excellence God demands when it comes to being truthful: "If it's not 100% truth, it's a lie." Try living life with this standard of truth.

I wrote the confession and sent it to nearly thirty people over a few months. Only three turned on me, cut off contact, and blocked me on Facebook. Not surprising to me at all, they were the three evangelists I knew. Everyone else not only accepted my apology but they all loved me in their responses, and our relationships grew and profoundly strengthened as a result. Several people in my acknowledgments, at the beginning of the book, were some of the recipients of that confession, including Tracy as she stated in her forward.

What I heard from everyone was that they admired my obedience and my desire, to be honest, and seek to please God in my life. I couldn't change my past, but I could walk a Romans 12 future in truth. He was changing me again, and I was so thankful for the changes. I just kept growing and learning how to truly find his peace. In the real world, my life was a disaster! My job was horrible and except for Tracy, I had yet to find one major relationship in my life that had not ended in abandonment.

Yet, God was equipping me and setting in me his strong foundation to love, serve and honour him and others on a level I didn't even know existed. As things got worse and more desperate for me, my refuge and strong tower got bigger in my life and heart.

Sadly, I now must share with you the worst attack of all. It took me years to overcome it, despite much prayer and the many months of Christian counselling at the time to help me cope with what they did to me. It was so severe, vile and evil that it took me to the very edge.

I've not made a personal comment about my abusers up until now because this is a book about God's love and part of that love is grace and forgiveness, two fundamental aspects of Jesus' love for me to seek and walk out in my life.

However, I would not honour myself if I didn't at least state for my sake that this was the most treacherous and malicious attack orchestrated by some very dark and lost souls in Christian leadership I have ever encountered. What they all did went against every loving thing Jesus ever did and preached and still troubles me greatly.

Chapter 24

"If I speak with human eloquence and angelic ecstasy but don't love, I'm nothing but the creaking of a rusty gate. If I speak God's Word with power, revealing all his mysteries and making everything plain as day and if I have faith that says to a mountain, "Jump," and it jumps but I don't love, I'm nothing. If I give everything I own to the poor and even go to the stake to be burned as a martyr but I don't love, I've gotten nowhere. So, no matter what I say, [no matter] what I believe, [no matter] what I do, I'm bankrupt without love." 1 Corinthians 13:1-7MSG

IN THE FALL of 2012, I sought out and joined a woman's group at a large church in the area. After a few weeks enjoying my time with the women, I decided to try out the service.

This was a much larger church than the last one but so positive and progressive. The messages online were very warm and positive, speaking about the unity in the church and brothers and sisters helping each other etc. The central theme of all his sermons was love and to be there for each other.

So, I went to my first Sunday service and was standing at the end of the row, near the back, enjoying the worship when suddenly a man I vaguely knew from the last church came flying up to me seething through his teeth as he spoke, "I'm not going to let you deceive them here too! You're not going to get away with it! You better leave now because I'm going to make your life a living hell!" He then turned and marched off into the lobby and began to grab ushers while pointing at me. He waved his arms wildly while throwing me very menacing looks. He spoke to me with the same demonic voice from the movie The Exorcist. It was as if a demon was speaking through him. All he needed was to spin his head around and spit pea soup at me to make it complete.

(I came to find out much later, that the last church, after my departure, had sent six men out separately to go from church to church every Sunday looking for me so they could warn the leadership about me.)

I remember sitting down shaking because his menacing words disturbed me greatly.

The music eventually came to an end as I tried to shake off the violence of his words. I also noted he was standing eight feet directly behind me, leaning on the wall keeping an eye on me.

The pastor, let's call him Bill, was fantastic. He was so loving and so kind, he was warm and really cared. I found that he really spoke to me. By the end of the service, I knew that I could talk to him and let him in on my story and hopefully find a loving community to help me heal. So I approached him and told him I needed to speak to him, and it was important.

We met alone, and I told him my story. At the end, he thanked me then asked me for the name of the church I just left. I wouldn't tell him, but he insisted and spoke about positive closure. He was so positive and gentle that I relented and told him. He thanked me with a genuine reassuring look that said not to worry, and we parted with his assurance that he would keep what I said to him confidential and that I would find love there and that I was welcome.

A week later I got an email from Bill requesting that I come to his office and meet with himself, the two pastors from the last Church who interrogated me, and his regional pastor for the area. After my hesitant response indicating that I wasn't about to be interrogated by those two again, he reassured me that this was his meeting and he would not allow it to get hijacked by the two pastors and that his goal was to have me part amicably with them. I agreed, and at four p.m. I met with all four in the church's boardroom.

It was all four on one side of the table and me on the other.

I was there for five hours!

This time, instead of the two pastors blocking the door and taking turns interrogating me, all four were at it. They kept asking me the same questions, just worded differently. Always about my relationship with Sarah in the hopes to trip me up in a lie. Also, they tried to convince me that the devil had my soul and that I needed to be, 'The man God made me to be.'

At one point while defending myself, I mentioned that I have an 'F' on my driver's license. The regional pastor asked if he could see it. So I got my license out of my wallet and slid it to him. He picked it up and looked it over intently, tilting it this way and that way, then said, "Huh, this is good. Who made this for you?"

I said the government.

He responded, "No, I mean, this isn't *real*. Who made this for you?"

I know what you're thinking. It was obvious that they ambushed me. All asking me the same sexual sin-based questions and working in unison. I just kept remembering Bill's sermons that talked about inclusive love for all.

You have to appreciate that I was so desperate for someone to care about me and help me heal, unfortunately, I was so messed up and weary by everything that was going on in my life to see the truth about them. I had done nothing wrong, but it seemed that this didn't matter. They were going to get their pound of flesh.

A week later I met a couple at church who introduced themselves to me and offered to take me to lunch. After a short time, we became friends, and I shared my story with them as God had told me to; which they were fine with.

A few weeks later, I was asked to meet with Bill and the associate pastor in this couple's home. It was there that I was informed that all washrooms were permanently off limits to me. I was indefinitely barred from the women's ministry, volunteering, attending any church event, Bible study, or joining a small group. Basically, I could come to Sunday service, hand them my money then leave without peeing. This was put to me as what was required until they, 'got to know me better.'

Then, a month later just before Christmas, the couple that had befriended me, invited me to her parents' home way out in the country for dinner. Her father was a retired minister, and he was all over me with questions about my condition; apparently, her parents had been informed.

I came to find out later that he was told about me by Bill, and I was taken up there strictly in the hopes that this retired minister could rescue me from the devil and help me come to my senses and be, 'The man God made me to be.'

Chapter 25

"Do you who are Christians desire revenge and vindication? Just remember that Jesus Christ's death hasn't been revenged, nor his innocence vindicated!"

Saint Augustine [revised]

A FEW MONTHS later I was formally diagnosed with Partial Androgen Insensitivity Syndrome.

People have asked me if knowing that I have this condition helped me. Yes! In a huge way. It finally helped me understand what had happened to me. I must say, however, that the internet is jammed full of information on the common type, full or complete AIS but little is written on the partial version. It took much research on my part, including reading medical journals, to gain the understanding I now have.

It put a label on it for me but, it was mostly for the benefit of all those who insisted that I am a perverted man pretending to be a woman. I am so thankful to be able to say that I was born with it and that this is a genetic condition and not a perverted sexual lifestyle choice I made in my 30s that they all accused me of. To have proof to back it up was so exciting. Yet in the end, it didn't matter to any of them because they refused to believe me. They all still regarded me as a man in drag, deceiving myself and others.

I should have been vindicated with this diagnosis. But, not once, did they, *"look beneath the surface so they could judge correctly,"* as Jesus said in John 7:24 NLT

The definition of vindication is to show that someone who has been criticized or doubted is correct. What I said was true. I was female, and they had no right to vilify me. Yet, despite me sharing what I had recently learned about myself and the condition I was born with, it never stopped them.

One of them actually said to me, "Why is it that when sinners are challenged with the truth of their sin, they use the medical establishment to invent some new disease or condition so they can continue to justify their sin?"

Absolutely unbelievable! Here I had proof, including indisputable medical evidence, graphic photos of others with this disorder online and yet their response was; I just made it up to justify my sin!

So bizarre but those who refuse to believe that there is grey in the world will stop at nothing to keep their hearts hard and prove themselves correct as they pridefully refused to listen. Had my parents chosen female none of this would have happened but they didn't.

Not everyone turned on me, however. During my six months at the church, I had let several in on my condition, and I had been very much loved by them. Leadership might have been against me but not everyone.

Chapter 26

In the darkness, in the storm
When what is wrong won't bend
There is a right, there is a God
And one day, wrong will end.
There is a right, there is a light,
An answer, there will be,
I'm on my knees, I'm praying, please,
My Savior, unto Thee.

So now, we will not be afraid,
even if the earth is shaken,
If mountains fall to ocean depths;
And ground we've gained is taken,
Though seas may roar, though seas may rage,
and hills, by violence, shaken,
God is our shield,
We will not yield,
His answer will awaken.
                    Shannon Hanes

SIX MONTHS LATER, I was still barred from everything and pastor Bill would not communicate with me. Finally, I cornered him in the lobby. I mean I really had to corner him. He actually tried to dodge me more than once. I asked him about volunteering, and he lovingly smiled and told me that he'd check with the leaders in charge of that and get back to me.

Yeah, he lied.

A few weeks later, I was contacted by a few who were sympathetic towards me. They asked to meet with me because they needed to share with me all that they had uncovered, about a massive conspiracy against me.

"Jesus turned first to his disciples and warned them, "Beware of the yeast of the Pharisees—their hypocrisy. The time is coming when everything that is covered up will be revealed and all that is secret will be made known to all. Whatever you have said in the dark will be heard in the light and what you have whispered behind closed doors will be shouted from the housetops for all to hear!" Luke 12:1b-3 NLT

We first talked about the very vicious email that was going around about me that each one of them had received. It was written by the professional evangelist from the last church who, to date, is the greatest fear monger I have ever known. It was genuinely libelous; full of lies and half-truths and spun in such a negative, vicious and slanderous manner, that it ensured that all that read it would run from me. Then they sadly informed me of all the other things that had been uncovered.

Pastor Bill never kept what I told him in confidence that first day I met him as he had promised. It turns out that over forty people in leadership positions throughout the church and their spouses were informed about me that same day and to be on the lookout for me if I sought to volunteer.

The leadership from both churches had joined forces that first week before my meeting with the four pastors. At an emergency closed-door meeting with the leadership from both churches present, it was decided that I was to be permanently barred from everyone and everything except Sunday service. I was never to be allowed to join the community.

Despite the outcry from a few in leadership to simply have me barred entirely from the church, it was hoped that in time I would either realize my sin and be, 'The man God made me to be.' or I would grow frustrated by the complete isolation and leave on my own; while to others, leadership would still appear loving. And if I complained publically, leadership would stand firm and united and make me out to be a wolf trying to divide the church.

I call it 'The Church Game.' Sad but I've read dozens of accounts of other Christians who shared this same testimony.

You see, churches cannot appear to turn people away. On the outside, they must look pure and loving to all but inside they can abuse quietly, and no one knows or believes it to be true of their leadership.

It was also determined that the couple that befriended me were enlisted by Bill to enter into my life for the sole purpose of spying on me. I wondered why the wife would suddenly leave our conversation in mid-sentence to ask me about having sex with Sarah. I suppose they were hoping I'd finally answer "truthfully" with her since it was obvious that I hadn't with them.

The meeting ended, and I was utterly demoralized. I couldn't cry for days after hearing the truth. I wanted to cry but I couldn't. I needed to so badly, but I was so distraught and numb that the tears wouldn't come. I was truly in shock and on the verge of a mental break.

Yet, what gave me great hope was that I had several seriously angry people who were furious at the church leadership for treating me with such utter contempt. Also, it wasn't 'Laura the crackpot' against the loving two-faced pastor and his staff spanning two churches and roughly eighty people. There were others with me. All of them, long-time members who had witnessed my backstabbing by Bill and his many friends from the shadows, all the while this same hypocritical pastor talked about unconditional love and absolute inclusion in the Christian community for all from the pulpit.

At this point, I left the church and vowed never to attend another church again! I was done with church. My faith in pastors was gone. My faith in Christian leadership was gone, and my faith that there was a church I could ever attend without being abused was also gone. God had charged me to share the truth about my life, and I knew what that meant for me in any church in future—isolation, pain, segregation, bigotry, hate and discrimination by those who say they follow Jesus.

I sat at home every Sunday for weeks, but I was cripplingly isolated and desperately in need of love and loving people. In the eight months that passed since the pastors barged into my house, I had been ridiculed, demonized, attacked, demeaned, made to feel shame for a genetic condition, called a liar and a perverted man in drag and everything else they could do and say to destroy me and take my non-existent self-esteem and crush it into the negatives.

I did however quickly seek counselling at this point because I was on the verge of a nervous breakdown. They had massively added to my pain without any regard for their actions!

I am certain to this day that the couple that drove me home still thinks I'm unsaved and that they are exempt from loving me. And that pastor Bill thinks he did everything correctly as he stabbed me in the back from the shadows.

The only positive thing to come from this whole affair was running into one of my supporters at Costco a few months later. She told me that the week after I left, she and her husband who sat in the second row center were listening to the pastor once again talking about loving our brothers and sisters and that we need to include all those who call themselves saved and that we need to love them no matter what and walk in love and unity.

She told me that she got so furious as he kept going on that she finally exploded. She stood and cut him off in mid-sentence screaming, "Except for Laura! You're nothing by a hypocrite!" She then turned and left the church never to return. She told me that her husband sat there dumbfounded then finally followed her out.

This wasn't to be my last encounter with these 'church people' from these two churches.

A few months later, one evening at Walmart, the professional evangelist and the author of that horrible email about me, ran up to me telling me that I was going to hell if I didn't repent or something of that nature. Not long after he started, I felt my anger welling up in me so I told him I was going to walk away before I said anything that would dishonour the Lord.

I turned my back to him and began to walk away to finish my shopping. Well, he got very incensed and began to shout so loud that everyone in this giant store could hear him. He shouted about how I was a man, and I needed to repent and be, 'The man God made me to be.' He went on and on. I was five aisles away, and he was still at it.

Sadly, I need to juxtapose this encounter with this one.

This is the same man who had myself and Sarah in his home when we first arrived. This same 'loving Christian' with a lovely wife and two beautiful children was so humble and caring to us. He was a deeply committed and passionate Christian, who I joined in prayer on many occasions at church, and yet, lacking even a drop of God's love. I don't knock him for it. At the time, I didn't have any of God's love either. In future chapters, I'll discuss what I mean by that.

Chapter 27

"Not everyone can accept this statement," Jesus said. "Only those whom God helps. Some are born as eunuchs," Matthew 19:11-12a NLT

I FINALLY NOTICED that when I shared my story with others, I kept strictly encountering two types of opposite Christians.

The first type are over the top gentle, peaceful and genuinely loving people, who are so sympathetic and caring to me. They seek to support me and hug me at every opportunity. The second are vicious, angry, aggressive, in my face and plotting my destruction. There didn't seem to be anyone in between.

What I did know was that there had yet to be even one evangelist who didn't take aim at my head with the biggest stone they could throw. Then one night I read the verse above, and it all made sense. That is the most accurate statement I have ever read about how I've been treated by my fellow Christians, and it came from Jesus himself! Eunuch and intersexed are basically the same thing. We are born with a body between genders.

I am convinced that how God 'helps them understand' is when he placed within a Christian his love. In doing so, they begin to see others through the loving and grace-filled eyes of Jesus. Sometimes it happens through great trials in their life, or it happens when he prompts us to see God's love in others, and we seek him for it. Or sometimes we're just gifted with it right from the start.

There is a huge difference between having God's love 'for' you and having God's love in you.

It's through having God's love in us that it allows us to understand. I am also convinced that if we are walking in our human understanding of love, we will stone others. I have yet to see different.

There is a great risk when we walk without his love in us. About a year ago, I sat in the break room at work, the day I shared my testimony as I described in the introduction. But what I didn't share in the introduction, was the conversation that began that facilitated her asking me my story.

She and I were talking when she said to me, "Yeah and 'them born agains.' They're the worst of all."

I smiled at her and said, "Judy, I am one of them born agains."

She responded loudly, "No you're not!"

I said, "Yes, I am."

"No, you can't be. You're not angry and violent and in-my-face like they are."

What was I supposed to say to that? 'Yes, I agree with you. Yes, you're right because they've been in my face far more than yours.' That's what she knew of Christians. Prideful, arrogant and haughty people, morally attacking everyone while sinning in their self-righteous judgement of others in the process.

She avoided them because she knew their true heart condition as I did. Her understanding of God and Jesus and those who follow him is based on angry people demanding that others follow in their black and white footsteps.

Not once in her life did anyone until she met me, meet her where she was. They all just pointed their haughty finger and screamed at her. This was her understanding of what 'them born agains' are all about. Anger, violence and hard hearts to everyone who don't agree with them 100%.

Sadly, there was no room in her thinking even to grasp that a Christian could be loving. Yet, she's not alone. When I used to go out and do street evangelism and lovingly evangelize to people, I never could tell them that I was, 'one of them born agains,' because they all had been abused by one already and would immediately shut down and back away from me quickly.

So, you must be wondering how I responded to her. Well, I told her that as with any group, there are immature and very mature people. I told her that we're all not like them. The immature attack and are vicious, and they are the ones people remember. The mature Christians don't attack or judge and have no interest in being in your face, except to love and accept you for who you are like I do. I told her that coming to Christ is a personal decision and one that she needed to make on her own and that I would be around if she wanted to know more. She then asked me how I came to Christ and I shared my testimony in a break room at the table with many others listening in.

I have yet to meet one unsaved person who doesn't universally understand born-again Christians as angry, violent and mean-spirited people, wanting to force their opinions on others.

This needs to change! I'll talk more in depth about this later.

Chapter 28

Do not dwell on the things you cannot change but dwell instead on the one who can make it happen.

A FEW WEEKS had passed since leaving the church, and I was still completely isolated except for my counsellor that I was seeing. I was still so fearful to return to a community of saints that seemed hell-bent on stoning me to my face or stabbing me from the shadows. I still hadn't dealt with my past, and now I had all new levels of crushing pain to deal with.

My only complaint to God was that he was insisting I take the high road and not sin against them but to remain meek and humble and walk out Romans 12 at all costs.

Yet, these so-called Christians could sin against me at will, viciously brutalize me, treat me like dirt, defy God's number one commandment to love me and do it all with absolute impunity, while grinning all the more by how much pain they could inflict on me.

I wanted them condemned for what they did! I questioned their faith and their salvation in my heart. That level of back stabbing, hypocrisy and deception were beyond what I thought anyone truly following Christ could do.

Yet God in response slapped me down hard!

He reminded me that what others do, or don't do, in *his* kingdom, is none of my business and that my job is to do his will without complaint or comparison. In essence, he told me to stop whining and that my own backyard had many weeds and to stop looking at other people's backyards despite their weeds hanging over my walls.

He gave me this verse to reinforce his position:

"Who are you to judge someone else's servant? To their own master, servants stand or fall. And they will stand, for the Lord is able to make them stand." Romans 14:4NIV

Oh, how I wanted to scream that verse at all of them to defend myself, but he wasn't going to let me judge them as they had judged me because I was walking in intense anger against them. Remaining silent and doing nothing in return, was what I needed to do so I wouldn't sin. But more than that, I knew I had to forgive them.

Yet, God never forced me to do that. I knew it was my choice. We have to choose to forgive from our heart, not our head; it's really for our sake. He won't push that on us because it's a heart choice, not a head choice. We can say we forgive but we must mean it and that can only come from the heart.

He did ask me to pray a blessing on them, however, (Romans 12:14) and that helped speed up the forgiveness process because it made me soften my heart to them. I will say that from practical experience, unforgiveness will keep our focus and heart anchored to our past. But God is in our future, and I've learned that it's best just to forgive, as he forgives me, so I can move forward in step with him in all he is doing for me. Ultimately, I left them all behind in that forgiveness and sought God for much better things to come.

Chapter 29

"But [Thomas] replied, "I won't believe it unless I see the nail wounds in his hands, put my fingers into them and place my hand into the wound in his side." Eight days later the disciples were together again and this time Thomas was with them. The doors were locked; but suddenly, as before, Jesus was standing among them. "Peace be with you," he said. Then he said to Thomas, "Put your finger here and look at my hands. Put your hand into the wound in my side. Don't be faithless any longer. Believe!""" John 20:25b-27 NLT

DURING THIS TIME, I often thought about taking one of the disbelievers into a bathroom and dropping my pants so they'd finally believe me that I had no ability to have sex with anyone, but God was vehemently against it.

First of all, I had done nothing wrong, and I knew in my heart that I was innocent. Secondly, it was none of their business for the same reason it was none of mine. (Romans 14:4) But more importantly; God was against it. Instead, God gave me these scriptures to help me understand his stance.

"Do not give dogs what is sacred; do not throw your pearls to pigs. If you do, they may trample them under their feet and turn and tear you to pieces." Matthew 7:6 NIV

This told me that my body was sacred to God that I was to cherish it and appreciate that God made me like this for a reason. I was valuable and loved by him. To expose myself in this way would dishonour the Lord and me. But not only that, their hearts were hardened against me, and no amount of proof would change their hearts. Even if I had shown them, they would have trampled on me anyway because they were pigs.

"When the Pharisees heard that Jesus had arrived, they came and started to argue with him. Testing him, they demanded that he show them a miraculous sign from heaven to prove his authority. When he heard this, he sighed deeply in his spirit and said, "Why do these people keep demanding a miraculous sign? I tell you the truth, I will not give this generation any such sign." Mark 8 11-12 NLT

Jesus knew they had plenty of opportunities to believe in him and yet the religious types kept demanding proof, even though his miracles were well documented. No matter what miracles he did, their hearts remained hard because to believe him would require them to surrender, let go of their pride and admit they were wrong.

He knew that their hearts would not change regardless of what he did or said because they walked in pride and self-righteousness. They showed up to argue with him, which speaks of immense self-righteousness and a haughty spirit and he wasn't about to oblige them.

In the same way, God said to me that no matter how many times I humiliated myself by showing someone my genitals, there would always be one more who demanded to look first-hand and ultimately they still wouldn't believe. Like the Pharisees, those who opposed me had hard hearts and no amount of evidence, even visual evidence, would dissuade them from believing the horrible things they thought about me.

You would think that I was finally done with these two churches for good, but sadly I wasn't. They had actually stepped up their attack by publically committing libel against me.

Chapter 30

*"I will not tolerate people who slander their neighbors. I will not endure
conceit and pride. I will search for faithful people to be my companions."*
Psalm 101:5-6a NLT

A MONTH OR SO after I left, I decided to visit this small church
near my home. They were all so friendly, and in a short time, I was
meeting people, attending Sunday school and doing my best to fit in.

About a month in, I sat down with Colin and Joy Cook, the pastor
and his wife and I shared my story with them. When I was done sharing
not only my story but all that had been done to me by the other churches
in the area, they looked at each other and smiled. Then he looked at me
and said, "I know you're going to find this hard to believe, but we've been
hurt by church people more than you have."

A pastor and his wife telling me they've been abused worse than me!
That statement floored me! He then informed me that the elders, his wife
and himself all independently had been informed by these two churches
to be on the lookout for me. He told me that he got an email from them.
I suspect that every pastor in the region got that same email.

I was in absolute disbelief. When would they stop?

They still haven't to this day.

In late 2015, I was contacted by a friend of Sarah's who had blocked
me on Facebook years earlier at the pastor's insistence. Yet, suddenly she

friended me. I allowed it and immediately in Messenger she began quizzing me about where I was and what specific church I attended. I knew her long enough to know that those weren't her words and that she wasn't doing the typing. They were searching for me. When I responded that I was in Toronto and I was unwilling to share what church I attended, she suddenly blocked me again mid-conversation, never to be heard from since.

Then last summer I received an email from the wife of one of the two pastors who abused me at the first church. In the email, she went on about me needing deliverance and ended it with a link to a radio broadcast where the topic was, 'Overcoming perverted sexual practices and finding wholeness by salvation in Christ,' or something of that nature.

I laughed when I received it, and I laugh now as I remember the email. Despite the truth and medical evidence to the contrary that I shared with them, she is still convinced that she's right about me and that I'm a sexually perverted man in denial.

I thought about just dumping the email and walking away. Yet, I knew that God wanted more from me. So, in the most loving way I could, I responded and told her that I didn't need to be saved because I already was. I reminded her about my condition and that everyone's understanding regarding me wasn't correct and that I will never see her again, so I have no motive to lie.

But again that verse from Mark 8 where the Pharisees are demanding of Jesus for yet another miracle popped into my head. I came to see that no matter how much I shared God's love and grace with her, in the end, she pridefully had to be correct and remain in the land of black and white.

"You should clothe yourselves instead with the beauty that comes from within, the unfading beauty of a gentle and quiet spirit, which is so precious to God." 1 Peter 3:4NLT

I tried with all that I had to write the most loving response and to be the woman God wanted me to be in that verse on the previous page. Yet, I knew it was no use. The true blessing from Colin and Joy was that they never responded to that email when I came to their church that first week. He said that the email was spiteful and mean-spirited, so he chose to ignore it. He told me he was so glad that I trusted them enough to tell them first-hand and that they believed me. They were the nicest people and had chosen to give me a safe haven from the abuse. I just wish I had been better to them!

I was just so angry. At one point I really attacked Joy via emails and I also really gave Colin quite a time. Despite them knowing that my anger was a result of such brutal treatment and that 'hurt people hurt people,' they and many others suffered much because of me and in the end moved away from me for safety.

My anger was worse than ever, despite the counselling and it wasn't long before my angry tone, and sharp outbursts were being seen by many. I was deeply hurt, and I was acting it out in very damaging ways.

I was so conditioned to believe the worst in everyone, because every time in my past, for as long as I could recall, the people around me I trusted would attack me from behind. Every time I began to believe that people actually loved me, they'd turn on me viciously and participate in such vile sin against me.

Yet, this church treated me so kindly, and no one was against me at all! They had no intentions of hurting me. Quite the opposite—they were trying to love me so much! God help me, these people didn't deserve what I did to them!

May I take this opportunity to say to you all at this church how profoundly and deeply sorry I am. I was so hurt and angry. I ask you all to please forgive me, especially you Joy. I am so deeply sorry to you.

It wasn't intentional on my part, but I had massive feelings of injustice that were manifesting themselves in highly inappropriate ways. Plus, after so many years I still hadn't begun to work through all that my parents had done. I was just trying to cope with the latest church attacks. I am also thankful to this church for giving me a safe haven and for Colin and Joy. I truly wish I could have done better. I was just so completely screwed up.

The last week I was in New Brunswick I sat down with Colin, and he asked me a question. He said that when I first met him, I told him that my faith in the position of pastor had been destroyed. He asked me how he did in repairing it. I said that it was better, but it would take an enormous amount of time and positive experiences before it would be repaired.

It was a short-lived time with Colin and Joy and this church, as by December 2013 I was moving back to Toronto for a new job. By the time I left Moncton, despite the counselling, I had no outlet to share and find a community to help me heal. So, as I moved back to Toronto, things would not end for me. There was still one more pastor and his assistant who were hell-bent on abusing me, and it started before I had even been to my second service.

Chapter 31

"It is good when you obey the royal law as found in the Scriptures: "Love your neighbor as yourself." James 2:8NLT

UP UNTIL NOW I've not mentioned the churches I've attended. However, this church is so well-known for its unique ways that there's no way to share what happened at this one without many knowing what church I'm talking about. I won't alter my story, however, despite my desire to give those who abused me anonymity that may not be possible here and for that I'm sorry.

I began watching this church based in North Carolina online in early 2013. The teaching pastor is a highly charismatic and dynamic teacher. Absolutely led by the spirit! What a blessing his teachings were, and still are to me.

I knew they had a Toronto campus and I dreamed for months of attending this amazing church myself. Then suddenly I was moving to Toronto, and I could finally participate. This church is very high on volunteering and helping in the community, and they encourage people to volunteer immediately when you come.

In December 2013 I attended my first Sunday there, and it lived up to everything I could ever have imagined. I was given the opportunity to join a small group and to shadow someone volunteering the following Sunday so that I could become a volunteer immediately. I was signed up for the volunteer course a few weeks out in January, as well as the history of the church. That first Sunday I was so excited! I had watched them for so long online, and now I was part of it.

The following weekend was the massive ice storm that hit the entire region, so church was cancelled. A few days later, I met with the campus pastor's assistant and her husband because I wanted to share my story just so they'd know. But more, I wanted to share how excited I was to be there.

At the end of the meeting she abruptly cut short, she informed that I was not to shadow the following Sunday or join a small group. She basically told me to do nothing until told differently.

Four weeks went by and no word from her. Volunteer training was coming up so I asked her if I could now go. She said that I wasn't to take the training and still not join a small group. I asked her why but she refused to say.

Even though every week the pastor stood on stage and was begging people to volunteer and firmly insisted that we all attend a small group, I wasn't allowed to do either, and no reason was offered. The situation deteriorated because the more I asked why I was being barred from basically everything, without any reason or justification, they began calling me a troublemaker and spread that lie to all the staff.

I was perplexed because I had done nothing wrong and it seemed my only crime was asking why they were doing this. I hadn't even been there for two services, and I was barred from everyone and everything except the service itself and handing them my money of course.

At the same time, I made friends with a church leader in one of the campuses in North Carolina. In one of our phone conversations, I asked her why they were doing this.

She asked me if I have a criminal record. I said no. She stated that they only stop a person from volunteering for a time if they learn that the person applying has a criminal record, but she stated that this is dealt with quickly and nearly all in a week or two can then volunteer. She stated that they have many convicted felons volunteering without any oversight. It usually requires someone in authority sitting down with them and getting to know them a bit. She asked me if they had done this. I said that they refused to talk with me at all.

 She was at a complete loss to know why they had barred me before I had even been to my second service and that the church as a whole had no procedural reason to do that to me. She struggled to believe me because she had never seen or heard of such a thing.

She also sought her authority, keeping the inquiry vague and they too indicated that they too had never heard of this and that there was no reason for a campus pastor to do this without serious cause. In fact, one of the four tenants of the church is that all need to volunteer, so to block anyone from serving was only done in extreme circumstances because it went directly against what the church stood for.

I knew then that I had been barred because of the condition I was born with. They wanted me to leave right from the start and hoped that when I got frustrated at not being allowed to participate in the community at all, I'd go. They began, 'The Church Game' with me week one but I would not give them the satisfaction. I stayed and walked out those verses in Romans 12 like I was Christ himself and it was driving them crazy! Every time they did something to get under my skin, I responded with love. I also had made a friend with a very high up in this campus. She was one of the original people in Toronto who petitioned the main church to start the campus.

Every week I saw her she kept pushing me to join her small group, but I kept saying no. Eventually, I broke down and shared with her that I was barred. She asked me why and I told her that the pastor and his assistant refused to give me a reason. She said she would talk to them and she did.

After she did, she told me that they would not discuss it with her.

Then a few weeks later, she was now asking me why I wasn't volunteering or getting involved in any way. I broke down and told her everything regarding my condition and what they were doing to me. I made it clear that it was simply a matter of prejudice and intolerance on leadership's part and that this began week one.

What profoundly surprised me was that she believed me without question and apologized on behalf of the entire church for what was being done to me. I knew that was the Holy Spirit's doing, and I was thankful for it. She told me she was going to get to the bottom of this, so she requested a meeting with her, me, the pastor and assistant. She had set it for Sunday after church to finally work this all out and help bring us together in unity.

The night before the scheduled meeting, she called me and apologized that there would be no meeting. She said that the campus pastor had called her and had threatened her to stay out of it or and I quote her words, "They will do to me what they are doing to you." She apologized and backed right out.

Wow! That was extreme. What were they so afraid of? I was astonished. I had tried to join this amazing church that excited me so deeply. I was so on fire with the teaching and the desire the church had for serving in the community. I was so frustrated and felt such heartache by their actions. I had documented proof in the form of emails that clearly showed the bigotry. My friend in NC gave it to someone very close to the top of the church. The documentation was irrefutable proof that I was being truthful and that blatant discrimination was taking place.

Yet, it fell on deaf ears. It was obvious that they were going to back their bigoted campus pastor because he was one of the founding couples that started the church in NC in the beginning. Who was I? Just a crackpot to them, even with documented proof.

This wasn't the entire church campus itself but only the pastor and his assistant who led this campaign to turn people against me. They were doing their best to hurt me, yet, I was responding with Romans 12:14 and sought God for strength and protection.

Ultimately, I had to leave, because the two of them called me the following week and told me that I wasn't welcome and I was never to set foot in the church again. Surprisingly, I wasn't so much angry with the pastor and his assistant but that I had been so excited to be a part of this church and that it wasn't to be. I was pleased that throughout the ordeal I honoured them at every turn.

About two years later I told someone locally his name and what he did to me. She knows him on a professional level and found it unbelievable. Had she not known me for being very honest, she would not have believed it possible of him. He's all sugar and nice, just like Pastor Bill who smiled at me while stabbing me in the back.

In the face of all this, who would not be entirely cynical of church people and especially church leadership? I had the truth about my condition; I was born with a genetic birth defect! My setting things correct with my gender was a matter of survival for me! How was that possibly my fault or sinful in any way? Why was I being segregated and treated like a leper for being truthful about something I was born with, that my parents got wrong; that I set right?

One thing was for sure, I was done telling anyone anymore. I didn't care what God said; I was done talking about my condition!

Chapter 32

So, how is life in the Grey Zone?

IT WAS APPARENT to anyone who met me that I had issues and they were bigger than anyone wanted to help me with.

That's actually a widespread response; not wanting to get involved. I don't know how many times people told me to seek counselling when I turned to them, not for an ear but for a hug and some Christian love. Yet, they would harden their hearts and diplomatically suggest I go seek the advice of a professional while running from me as fast as they could.

Even in the past two years, I had one person insist that I go see a psychiatrist and a second person insist that I have a mental disorder and to go see a professional as well. They both made it a condition of being friends with me. Well, needless to say, I'm not friends with either. The only mental disorder I suffered from was, *'being kicked in the ass, just once too many times by trusted people'* disorder.

I didn't need to talk, I needed love. Hate and indifference by others had created in me so much pain and anger, and it would be God's love through others that would set me free. Yet, I couldn't articulate that because I hadn't figured that out yet.

I was so lost emotionally, and I felt so small. No one wanted me since I was a tiny child and it was just repeating itself, over and over. I had no chance to live a normal life.

All I wanted were hugs and affection and people who cared and loved me, and a partner to do life with. It seemed that I could never let people know me entirely because they only seemed to like me when I held back the truth and my pain. Ultimately, they only wanted to know me as an acquaintance but no more.

Was I looking in the wrong place for love? I'm sure I could have had plenty of secular friends who would love the socks off me and help me overcome so much. Was it unreasonable to want to be open and completely real and seek love from those in my own Christian tribe?

I was born in the grey zone, and that makes black and white Christians uncomfortable. This condition would forever require me to live in the grey zone and set me apart from everyone. It has made many Christians around me very uptight and angry because their understanding about the binary sex of men and women, per Genesis, wasn't only challenged by me but I'm a walking testimony to the inaccuracy of that black and white truth they cling to. Even Jesus saw that some aren't born men or women, as per the verse I shared earlier in Matthew 19, and this is not Eden!

There are even some churches that won't baptize or give communion to those like me, because if God only created men and women, then those born in between aren't part of God's creation and therefore aren't eligible to be considered human in God's eyes. In essence, they believe that I am disqualified from salvation because I am not entirely male or female physically and therefore I'm not one of his children.

Living in the grey zone is like standing outside in the snow and looking in the window of a home to see a loving family, caring for one another and sharing life together and knowing you will never be able to join in or form that family of your own. It's to live in the shadows outside in the cold, hopeless and in total isolation and despair, knowing you will never escape.

It's knowing that you're destined never to be invited in.

There are so many things that living in the grey zone takes from you beyond love and hope. It's the small things, like the fact that I have never tucked a child into bed or read them a story. Receiving a genuine and loving hug from a little one, that tells you in the hug they gave, that they appreciate and love you. So many things you take for granted that I will never know like giving birth to my own children or even just dating someone and knowing that they won't be repulsed by me.

I see so many families near me, even now and wonder what it would be like to be invited to sleep over on the couch Christmas morning and enjoy the kids getting up and the utter glee and excitement as they open their gifts. Helping them put some together and playing with them and just enjoying a warm family Christmas morning. For a brief moment to know what it's like to be part of a family and to enjoy a loving dynamic time that is so magical through the eyes of a child. It's a time that would propel me out of the grey zone. It can't be permanent but would bring me such joy, hope and memories that would keep me going when the isolation of the grey threatens to crush me.

I do get invited to Christmas dinners, but that's not the same as being an honorary family member like Great Aunt Laura who comes to stay with us every year. I pine to have my own kids. Heck, I'm old enough to be a grandmother, and yet that will forever be off limits for me.

The grey zone is a place of isolation and sadness, extreme loneliness and desperation. It's not where "normal people" reside but where those who don't belong are put. Like in the children's Christmas special, the island of misfit toys, those in the grey zone are misfits and unloved, not part of anything and left to be forgotten. Yet, because of this truth, those who live life in the grey zone are the ones Jesus sought the most to give his love and hope to.

Chapter 33

Living Life in the Grey Zone and John Chapter 9

PLEASE HEAD TO your Bible and read this chapter before you read further. I'm going to refer to things without verse citation, so it's best that this chapter is fresh in your mind. It also demonstrates issues at the core of this book, so please read the chapter in your Bible first to fully appreciate what I'm going to share. Please don't skip it.

It's not a stretch to know that this blind man at an early age knew that he lived in the grey zone. Because of his congenital birth defect, the Pharisees felt they knew the truth about him; that he was a sinner from birth and made him an outcast in his society. Yet Jesus said they were wrong. It was no sin he or his parents did that made him this way.

Not only did Jesus speak the real truth about this man and pointed out their error regarding him, he went even further to say that this man was made this way so the power of God could be seen through him!

What would that mean to the Pharisees and what did that mean to the disciples hearing that? Jesus took a man who was an outcast in his own religious community, or perhaps at best a tolerated sinner from birth and said that God's power is to be seen in him.

Please recognize the black and white, hard and pride-filled hearts of the Pharisees here. Then compare those same hearts to those in my church leadership who abused me. They took a man born with a congenital birth defect as I was and cast haughty sin-filled judgment upon him. Look at verse 18. They were so desperate to be right that they couldn't allow themselves to believe that he could see.

I can imagine standing there as this man looking at them saying, "Hello, I can see you. I'm not blind anymore!" With them responding, "No, we're sorry, but the truth is that you're a blind sinner from birth and if that doesn't work, we're going to rid our church of you because you upset our prideful, simple and comforting understanding of the real truth with the notion of grey."

I imagine through my own life experiences how this man could have been so bitter. Hearing others celebrating their young children, while his parents disowned him. Hearing families playing and enjoying life together as he sat alone year after year hearing the world pass him by. In time, he would have just existed without hope, knowing that no one loved him or cared about him because he lived in the grey zone.

Then imagine one day he heard men talk about him like he wasn't even there. The disciples already knew the truth about him as well and called him a sinner. Yet, did they talk to him? Did they get to know him before judging him and asking Jesus who sinned?

I wonder what the man thought when he heard Jesus say that it wasn't his fault and that no one sinned. Don't you think that over time he would have bought into this lie others told him was the truth? That in the end, he would have accepted that he was unworthy to be with others because God made him a sinner from birth, and that over time he would have become his own worst critic as to why he shouldn't be allowed to be with anyone else, and that what others believed about him obviously must be correct?

Then Jesus shows up and tells others the real truth; that he's not a sinner at all! Imagine how obtuse and unbelievable it would have been to this man after all those years of repeating to himself the lie of being a sinner from birth.

132

When Christians stand in judgment of others, over time, those being judged begin to stand in judgment over themselves.

What's so damaging about that is that the truth Christians believe, in reality, is nearly always based on faulty perceptions. Then in the same way and with the same words, those who are being judged begin to judge themselves. This is particularly the case of words spoken over children.

Even when their accusers are no longer with them, the accusations and abusive words spoken, still reside in their hearts, going deeper and deeper into their core belief of who they truly are as their minds replay the words over and over.

Then Jesus heals him just like that!

Think about this, the man could see! Finally, he could be a full and active member of the community; no longer to live as an outcast on the fringes. He suddenly had a bright future and options he never had before. He could finally be treated as an equal. He could now get a job, get married, have kids and live a simple happy life in the community. He had finally found freedom! He could finally escape the grey zone and be loved.

Yet, on this same day, everyone turns on him and rejects him instead. The church kicks him out, and his parents publically disowned him. He is formally abandoned by the exact people who should have been celebrating with him the fact that for the first time in his life he was free to be normal.

His parents would have always felt great shame regarding him like my parents did. His parents would have most likely distanced themselves from him at birth as mine did in some regards. And yet, when he was made to see there was no celebration but just more isolation, abandonment, betrayal and pain. But despite that, Jesus in the evening leads him to the real truth - himself.

I Praise God that no matter what others think of us, or judge us for, Jesus is always ready with welcoming arms to show us his love and grace!

"Then Jesus told the now sighted man, "I entered this world to render judgment—to give sight to the blind and to show those who think they see [black and white thinkers] that they are blind." Some Pharisees who were standing nearby heard him and asked, "Are you saying we're blind?" "If you were blind, you wouldn't be guilty," Jesus replied. "But you remain guilty because you claim you can see." John 9:39-41 NLT

This just highlights the trouble with our hearts when we look at people through our own guilty and truly blind eyes and never allow the Holy Spirit to change us, so that we might come to see the real truth about others, through the loving eyes and heart of Christ.

For the Pharisees to admit that Jesus healed, threatened their comfortable and safe, black and white truth. It was as necessary for them to continue to call the sighted man blind and a sinner from birth, as it was necessary for the pastors who abused me to try to find some sin in me, that would allow them to justify their actions towards me.

These are stubborn and pride-filled hearts on display in this chapter as well as the hearts I encountered. I laugh and wonder what Linda from the first church would have done had she been there when the man was in the temple? Probably held the door open when they threw him out.

This was never going to be about celebrating the fact that this man in their community could now see, and praising Jesus that a miracle had been performed. No, all they wanted was be right at all costs, and no amount of proof was going to change their minds.

For all those church people who attacked me, God showed me that no amount of evidence would help them reconsider their faulty judgment of me. They too pridefully judged me guilty with absolutely no evidence and damaged me so deeply as a consequence. I told them point blank that they were hurting me and they simply gave me half-hearted apologies and just kept going.

Sadly "loving Christians" (and Pharisees) turn into vicious, heartless and hateful Christians, hell-bent on seeking to destroy all those who need the unconditional love of Christ demonstrated to them most of all.

Yet, as Jesus showed us in his own life, he sought to get to know, love, encourage and extend hope through himself to all who reside in the grey zone.

I remember my pastor in New Orleans one Saturday night service in 2009 began to muse out loud and I am convinced that it wasn't part of his sermon. This is my best recollection of exactly what he said.

"You know, I've been a pastor for thirty years. And when I started, everything was so black and white. But over the years I've come to see that there's a lot more grey out there than I ever imagined."

His tone in that moment was so subdued and humble. It's as if he learned and accepted that his understanding of things was so small and narrow and that over the years, God had, in some small measure, widened and deepened his understanding of the truth of God's creation. A very humbling place to be to know that you're really blind. But that's the exact place we need to be for God to finally help us truly see as he said in John 9:41

Interesting that I remember that comment so many years later, but it resonated with me so much that it became the basis for the title of this book.

In time, as a pastor, God placed his heart of love in him, and as he began to see life through Christ's eyes and in turn, his heart was shown what real love is. For me, until I too received his heart and began to see life through the eyes of Christ, I never understood why this same pastor had such a peaceful and gentle tone until now. He was at peace with the grey zone and embraced all those in it because of God's love in him.

I never really appreciated him at the time I lived there. He truly is a genuine gift to God's kingdom and those in his church.

Part 4

My journey to wholeness

Chapter 34

"There is likely peace found nowhere else but resting in the Truth that God is great and He has a plan...a plan for each one of us that His hand made. May we all have true love and compassion for one another."
Debbie Tobler-Rydin

IN EARLY 2014 I began to attend a new church, but this time I kept my issue to myself. I was done with people turning on me. I vowed not to lie at all about my past, but I would not share anything either.

I held my emotions in to stem the tide of the volcano of negative emotions still within me. I just shut down and put on my game face. I was desperately lonely, but I knew if I shared my story, it would be the end of people being genuine, loving and real with me. If I shared the truth, the best I could hope for was to be treated with polite indifference. They would tolerate me there at best but the days of feeling loved and part of the community would end the moment they found out. Even if it didn't happen at all, I wasn't about to take the risk.

So I ignored God's standing order regarding sharing my condition, and I kept my mouth shut. And since I didn't talk about my past, I didn't have to lie about it.

In time, I began to hang around with the young adults. They are such a great group. They have time because they aren't weighed down by a spouse, kids and commitments. They have endless amounts of energy and are on fire for the Lord. So, after a few months, a group of young adults and me went to a revival about ninety minutes from the city one Saturday night.

It was a fine night, but I found that I was dry. I had not connected with the Lord for a long time, so my time that evening had been dulled. I tried to find him in the worship, where I typically find him but it seemed he was nowhere to be found. Eventually, there was an altar call to go up and let the Lord speak to you. So, I went up and sat in the front row, then I had this conversation with him.

"Do you trust me?"

"Yes Lord."

"No, you don't."

"But I do."

"Okay, prove it."

"How?"

"Tonight I am commanding you to tell this entire group your story."

"I can't."

"Why?"

"Because I can't bear to be hurt again."

"If you trust me, you will do this."

"Why?"

"Because, Laura, this isn't about telling them, this is about your trust in me no matter the outcome. Do you trust me?"

He asked me that question twice more, very loudly and then the conversation ended. He was dead serious, and I knew it. I had disobeyed him by keeping my story to myself, and he was calling me out on the fact that I didn't trust him anymore. It didn't matter what they did or said because I shared my story with them, this was between him and me. It wasn't about my story; it was about me not trusting him to take me into dangerous areas. Not sharing my story was based in fear and he was putting an end to it. I had to follow him fully, and he would settle for nothing less.

For me, it was as dangerous at it got, because things were going very well for me there. I was making inroads into the community and coming to prayer before the service and really joining in. This group embraced me because they knew how isolated I was. I had been invited out by them and that had not happened in years.

I had genuine community with them, and as I sat there in the front row pondering what could happen, I knew that I really had no choice. He didn't speak loudly to me often, so I knew that I had to obey him and tell them all my story.

So, over a late-night coffee, I shared my story with all eight of them. They were all fine with it except one young woman. She was having a real issue with it and kept insisting I tell the pastors. The others kept asking her why she was so agitated and upset. She just kept saying that the pastors need to be made aware of this. But we could all tell that she was against me. Several tried to probe her with questions as to what she was uptight about, but she would just continue to answer that the pastors need to know.

Every day after that, she would text me asking if I had told the pastors yet. She was truly in a panic.

A few weeks later I sat down with the three pastors and told them. They asked me a few questions, but they seemed to reserve comment. They weren't against me, but they weren't for me at all. It turned out to be the last time they were genuinely warm and friendly. From that moment on they were merely polite. They never went out of their way to attack me or hurt me, but any love and appreciation they had for me disappeared after that.

One of the pastors, a few days before I told them, saw me and gave me such a genuine hug. She said that she was so pleased to see me and that I was a welcome and wonderful addition to the church. Her hug and words were so warm, genuine and loving. She looked me in the eyes, and her affection was so visible. It was one of the most sincere and loving hugs I had received in easily a decade.

After I told the pastors, not only did she never hug me again, she physically kept her distance, staying a minimum of twenty feet from me at all times. She was polite and acknowledged me but was totally indifferent. She went from a physically loving and caring woman to a distant, closed and leery person when she saw me. Gone were the days when she would see me, move towards me and make a point of greeting me so kindly. Yet, all I did was share the truth. I hadn't changed, but she had, and so had the rest of the pastors.

As time went on, my best attempts to hold things in began to falter. Benign things said and done by others would cause me to massively overreact and strike first, as I drew on my pain and read everything as an all-out attack on me. I had a mountain of pain, and no one was going to add to it! I would protect myself at all costs.

Yet, not once did I read the signs correctly. I began making enemies of people who had done nothing wrong, and the slightest relational gaff on someone's part meant that I would launch a preemptive attack, then pull away from them and recede into myself for protection. This just kept happening, one slight by them at a time that turned into an all-out war against them, until there was no one left.

The young adults were such good friends to me, and they loved me regardless. Yet, in time, all that came to an end as well, as I had hurt them too. After my absence from the church for two months, with no one asking me if I was even okay in that absence, or where I was, I had come back to the church in the late spring of 2015 knowing that it was time for me to go when I was only met with stares, glares and angry looks from so many.

I was to blame for my having to leave. My anger and rage and so much else still enveloped my soul in a profound and real way. The emotions in me were reaching a crescendo, and I was just plain mad. Mad at everything and everyone. My tone was always argumentative. It's like the tone you hear in people when they are itching for a fight and you know they're just waiting for you to say something so they can 'go off' on you. Sadly, that became who I was. I was so bitter at the injustice and so mad at all that had been done to me.

I had demanded that everyone love me. I had demanded much from them, but it doesn't work like that. Demanding of others isn't a recipe for success. I never gave them a chance to get to know me. I wanted instant community access and genuine, deep and real friends but when that didn't happen, I felt betrayed. They gave love freely to everyone else, but they all seemed to keep it away from me. Yet, that wasn't really the case, it's just that I had hurt them all so badly over time that they didn't have it to give me.

My demanding had pushed them away, and for many, they closed off communication with me to stop me from hurting them anymore. I don't blame them at all. I was distraught and lost, and I demanded love from people who couldn't give me what only God could give me. I had destroyed so many over time by trying to attain something I couldn't get from them in the first place.

I was jealous of the very open love that these church members had for each other, yet even more frustrated and angry that I was not welcome to join in. I was also jealous of the families around me. The love of family is unique, and that bond is exclusive to its members, usually reserved for the ones that marry into the family; very few are invited in. It's the plight of living in the grey zone. Some days, even now, I yearn for that in my life. It's the normalcy of family unity in love that I have never had.

Young singles, without family or a spouse, understand this but generally, in time, they can build a family for themselves. They may feel themselves to be in the grey zone for a time, where despair resides but they really aren't.

W.I.S.H. stands for 'What I Should Have.'

I wish I was normal, but God chose to make me this way so his power could be seen in me. If that weren't the case, so many Christians around me would not have encouraged me to write my story that God used to change them for as long as they did.

Chapter 35

Therefore, accept each other just as Christ has accepted you so that God will be given glory. Romans 15:7 NLT

I WAS MADE this way so you could, while reading this book determine your own heart condition. How are you feeling about me? I have a derivative of one of the top five intersex conditions. I know you've probably heard the term intersex and for many in our tribe, they think, 'lost depraved lifestyle choice.' Or for some even worse, 'God's disqualified people.'

Yet, do you have a love for me?

Stop and consider this next question carefully.

Do you have Jesus' unconditional love for those who know themselves to be transgendered?

How are you with that?

For me it's simple, I think, 'Who am I to say what's right or wrong for them because only God knows the real and complete truth.

Yet, does it really matter who's right or wrong? Are we not to unconditionally love all as Jesus did as a Christian response?

Transgendered people live life in the grey zone as well.

As someone said to me at one point when I didn't know I had PAIS, "Laura you're a woman. No one would go through the amount of crap you've gone through if you weren't."

Transgendered children know who they are! Yet so many Christians blame the parents and say that the kid is just confused, in essence asking who sinned—the child or the parents? (John 9:3) Yet, the child knows who they are. It's those unloving angry Christians saying it who are the confused ones because, despite the aggressive attacks by some in our tribe, these young people never waiver and never back down from speaking out about who they know themselves to be. For them, it's a matter of survival as it was for me.

One of the greatest proofs offered in Christianity about the reality and sincerity of Jesus is that when he departed us, the disciples continued to claim things about him even when they were abused and aggressively attacked. The consideration is that no one would go through the amount of crap they went through for a lie. If Jesus wasn't who they claimed, they would have walked away when the abuse started.

We all can appreciate this logic to show the validity of the deity of Christ. Yet, we refuse to allow that same logic to apply to the transgendered individuals and intersexed for that matter, who have endured horrendous abuse by Christians and have not wavered in knowing who they are, despite all attempts to demonize, marginalize or segregate them out of their community unless they conform to a set of black and white norms.

You have read in this book attack after vicious attack and yet, not once was there any doubt in who I know I am, or any doubt in the pride that prevented my Christian abusers from appreciating the grey zone.

Remember what the Christians in California said about me? They knew the truth that I was a woman. There was no doubt in their minds. They saw the woman behind my male façade and celebrated with me when I let go of the male lie. They knew my femininity to be real and correct. So why is one group in our tribe right about me and so many others not?

Why was that mom of the five-year-old with PAIS correct about the violent Christians around her child? Having deemed it necessary to move out of state if they needed to reset their Childs gender correctly because the Christians in her community were ready to pounce on anyone who is different and especially one who has a genetic condition that involves the genitals or gender?

Having an insensitive heart, still allows God to help a person become sensitive in time. Reading a book like mine, or knowing someone with a similar condition and walking in their footsteps for a time, as you have with me, brings the insensitive heart to a place of love and genuine appreciation of their suffering.

Being prideful, however, breeds indifference, bigotry, a desire for walls and borders and a desire to hold to their black and white understanding of truth and consider all those who don't, liberals, lost, or depraved.

In a climate of wall-building in the United States, where does that leave those in the grey zone? I have seen so many recent newscasts about those who live in the grey zone and the desperate fear they have regarding what brutality will be done to them by those who pridefully only see black and white. Yet, Jesus saw, recognized and embraced the grey zone and calls those who can't, the guilty and blind! (John 9:41)

I pray that as you read what happened to me, you will see that as the Christians were told about my condition, they became instantly and fearfully opposed to me. That isn't the loving heart of Christ; that's the heart of a Pharisee!

Recently I had someone near me demand that all transgendered children be barred from treatment until they are 25 – in essence, removing any chance to set their gender correct at a time when it's only effective. Not only were they condemning those children with a haughty and prideful tone to a lifetime of misery, this person wanted to force their personal opinion and addenda on these kids with an attitude of, 'I know the truth and what's best for them.'

They spoke with a pride and self-righteous haughtiness that sounded just like those who attacked me. I had to I wondered when this person was going to change their mind about me and turn on me next?

25 years ago, we didn't have the correlated evidence about my condition they have now regarding brain development and gender. If they would be wrong in attacking me back then, knowing what we know now, then why are they so sure they're 'right' in attacking transgendered individuals now?

Here's a question for you. Do you look at the heart of others or judge the outward? Notice below that God does not judge in this verse only the humans do that.

"The Lord doesn't see things the way you see them. People judge by outward appearance but the Lord looks at the heart." 1 Samuel 16:7b NLT

I need to be clear, this book is not about my condition or being a champion for anyone's rights. Instead, I was made this way so I could uniquely speak to my Christian tribe about our Christian hearts and to ask this one overarching question that millions of unbelievers and people abused by Christians like me have asked.

Why do Christians judge and attack others, when Jesus who knows the complete truth about everyone never has?

I think this statement below holds much of that answer.

The only real and lasting divide between people is the one we are pridefully unwilling to cross.

If you've been humbly changed by this book to the reality of grey in our world, then I praise God for his work in you. And I hope it empowers you to speak up and take a stand against those prideful Christians who are not walking in God's love and grace with regards to others who reside in the grey zone.

It's not a matter of 'truth' or right or wrong, for them or for us. It's a matter of loving as Christ did and leaving the judging behind. We must seek him to be 'all in' and to walk with his heart of love!

When we let go of our fleshly and faulty perceptions of the outward in others and see their heart as we pick up his cross, we can then love as Jesus loved.

Yet, some of you are probably saying, "Well, that's just your opinion Laura." No, actually it's not my opinion at all; it's Jesus' opinion.

When we are purchased by Christ, we are required to give up our personal opinion and must only take our master's opinion. None of us get a personal opinion about anything or anyone if we are following the son. It's his opinion that matters and his opinion we need to embrace in our heart and share as I am here.

I find that when we truly follow him, there is great peace that comes from that because we truly walk behind Jesus as we let go of our pride, haughtiness, personal opinions, worldly fears and prejudices of others, and instead, fully embrace Jesus' loving opinion of others instead.

When we seek this in our life, God helps us to rise above all these things that the enemy uses to drag us down and pit us against each other so we can begin to see others through the eyes of his son and to see beyond the outward in others to see their hearts, and in turn appreciate a bigger picture – Jesus' glory and love for us all. It is in that elevated godly perspective that we see everyone as a gift from God like Jesus does as we humbly receive his love in us to share with everyone in this world.

However, just like the Pharisees, many Christians choose to keep prideful and haughty hearts, as they judge others. It's a huge cost to the lost when we choose to hold onto our personal opinions, because when Jesus' supposed representatives are angry, vicious and judgmental, the lost will never come to know the love of Christ because the lost come to believe that Jesus is all about hate and violence, so they turn away from the one who loves them the most!

It's only when our hearts, minds and attitude genuinely becomes one of grace, love, peace and gentleness for everyone, as it is with Jesus, that the lost will find hope, love and his grace through us and come to know the love of Christ for themselves directly.

I guess the ultimate question we need to ask ourselves is, 'Do I have Jesus' heart of love in me? A love based on absolute unconditional love for all. A love that sees their heart and doesn't judge the outward in others, and a love that will draw the lost to Jesus.'

Here's a verse about the perspective we need to have.

"Since you have been raised to new life with Christ, set your sights on the realities of heaven, where Christ sits in the place of honor at God's right hand. Think about the things of heaven, not the things of earth. For you died to this life, and your real life is hidden with Christ in God. And when Christ, who is your life, is revealed to the whole world, you will share in all his glory." Col 3:1-4 NLT

Chapter 36

"Letting go is one of the major cornerstones of being liberated from your past. If you are ready to be set free, make a decision to release whatever is holding you back. Don't hang on to anything that is not empowering you to move forward. In reality, you always have the option of choosing whether you will focus on a hurtful past or fill your mind with uplifting thoughts of the present and all its blessings" Sue Augustine

AFTER A TWO-MONTH absence, I came to church, but instead of sitting up front where I generally sat, I sat in the back row because I knew no one wanted to see me. I was like the ex-wife showing up uninvited to my ex-husband's wedding rehearsal dinner. Everyone was indifferent to me and did their best to be polite, but it was easy to see that I wasn't welcome there.

There was a visiting pastor there that week, and at the end of his sermon, he had an altar call for those who needed emotional healing from traumatic life events. Hello! That's me! So, I went forward before he even finished asking and I sat in the front row and was now surrounded by irate bitter people who didn't want me there at all.

As the pastor began to pray on others who had come forward, the young woman who had accompanied the visiting pastor came over and knelt before me.

She had such a loving, positive and caring spirit that I shared with her in tears that I had destroyed so many people in the church. I then gave her a thirty-second outline of my story as the weight of my sorrow in hurting so many enveloped me. I said it seemed that every time I wanted to move forward, I ended up going further back and I was so desperate to stop hurting others and yet I couldn't stop doing it.

Well, she began to pray for me, and after a short time, she started to speak prophetically into my life. She was speaking with absolute authority as she spoke of a bright future where I would be set free and be made whole.

In the middle of my darkest valley and surrounded by those I had made my enemy by the hurt I had done to them, God had shown up through this young woman to let me know it wasn't over and that there was still hope for me that one day I would be made whole. One day I would stop hurting others and demand of them. One day people would see me as a joy to be around and not someone to avoid. I would light up a room when I entered it, as opposed to lighting up the room when I left it.

We talked some more after the prayer, so by the time we were done most everyone had departed. Eventually, I got in my car and began to drive home.

On the way home, I started repeating this sentence: "Your faith and trust in God can set you free." I just kept repeating it but it wasn't me saying it, it was the Holy Spirit. I didn't even notice right away. I have no idea how long that sentence kept repeating before I noticed I was saying it. But when I did notice, I couldn't stop saying it. He was speaking to me, through me and because I couldn't receive it, he just kept repeating it. Eventually, I started to actually listen and ponder this sentence: "Your faith and trust in God can set you free."

As I began to tune in and begin to believe, the sentence immediately changed to: "Your faith and trust in God WILL set you free."

This was so hard for me to accept and receive. I was beyond hope and such a menace to everyone. By leaving this church, I was 'saving them from me.' But this time I was making that call. How could I ever get set free? I had given up hope of ever being in a community of believers that loved me and where I didn't hurt everyone.

One church after the next, and a stream of innocent and damaged people in my wake. I was leaving this church as well, but God kept telling me that my faith and trust in him will set me free.

Eventually, over a few minutes of that sentence repeating itself, knowing that it was God saying it and that it was my reality if he was saying it, I let go of the self-pity I was gripping onto, and I received it. Then, as the truth of this sentence became a reality in my heart, the next sentence to be repeated was my own: "MY faith and trust in God will set me free." This time it was me repeating the sentence, not the Holy Spirit.

At this point, the realization that there was hope for me embraced my heart as the tears began to really pour out of me. In those tears, something was happening to me. I felt the anger and rage, and all those negative emotions start to go. I was desperate to see them go and it was as if they were slowly draining out of me and the more I cried, the more they were being flushed out as I continued to repeat those words, "My faith and trust in God will set me free. My faith and trust in God will set me free."

But it was a joyful, refreshing flow of tears, not a lamenting type. It was as if, for the first time in my life I was holding my baby girl I had just given birth to, and the tears would not stop coming as I sobbed. I was so overwhelmed by the beauty of God's creation I was holding in my arms, looking at that tiny little face and praising God for her.

For me that day, these were cleansing tears, and in that moment, I was being changed by God as his love, mercy and joy invaded my damaged heart and soul. He was cleansing me with his own radiance and love, and I was so overwhelmed. It was then that I knew within myself that things had profoundly changed in me. There was no doubt at all when I began to speak this last sentence: "My faith and trust in God HAS set me free!"

I was healed! I was set free. The anger I held against my parents and the doctors and all who abused me growing up—gone! My anger, frustration, shock, outrage and bitterness for every church and every person who abused me—gone! I was healed! I was set free and so full of joy in that moment. He had taken all the negative within me, and he had replaced it with his peace. It wasn't an onion layer with more bitterness to be uncovered later; IT WAS ALL GONE!

It was the moment he opened my heart and placed his love within me to now see others through the eyes of Christ. Suddenly, I was unable to hate or even dislike.

In that moment, he gave me the heart of real and lasting forgiveness and so much grace. I knew that I loved them all as I finally understood Christ so much more. His gentleness and his love for others was so deep and real in me now. Jesus held no malice, bitterness, or anger for anyone but only looked at the Pharisees with love. He couldn't look at them any other way and now neither could I!

Andrea, the woman who spoke over me, had spoken prophetically in church as to what was about to happen that same day. I had been set free! But more than that, I had his heart to love and forgive in me! It was so overwhelming and to be honest as I write this; it still is! How I don't deserve to know this love so intimately. It's a great gift and one I know that I cannot sit on.

James MacDonald said, 'God's love isn't made complete when we receive it but when we give it to others.' That day I understood the depth of that statement. I had in my human ability tried to walk love out, yet in reality, I didn't have God's love in me. I had his love 'for' me but not 'in' me. That is a massive distinction.

I wrote that the evangelist who shouted at me at Walmart didn't have his love and yet neither did I. He knew God's love for him, but it wasn't in him. I know that's a bold statement and you must be thinking how do I know that. But I've encountered so many Christians since that day who walk in God's love, and it permeates their essence of who they are. It becomes your identity and in time everything you think, say, believe and do is about Jesus; love, grace and peace. It releases you from the binds of our human issues and troubles. You begin to see everything and everyone through the eyes of a loving God, and in that moment you find absolute peace. It makes walking out Romans 12:9-17 easy. Not in a cocky human sense do I say easy but it's 'easy' because God's love in you makes it easy. It was in that moment that I was able to love my abusers, really love them and pray blessings on them and mean it with all my heart. To know and picture myself hugging them, every one of them and having such love for them!

I still had a long journey ahead, but for the first time, there was hope for me as I was made whole. I had massively underdeveloped social skills and no self-esteem. I spent so many years having Christians knock me down and kick me as well that I was still reeling from the mental and emotional abuse and the automatic attacking reactions that came out of me as a result.

For so long, I prayed and hoped that I would find someone to actually believe in me and have faith in me. To speak life and light into my heart and encourage me to succeed because they would keep telling me that I was worth it.

But God didn't send just one, he sent a group! I was about to meet Christians who would show me what God really thought of me. They showed me his heart for me, and they helped him reprogram the very core of my soul. It wasn't just about healing from the hurt, God needed to show me the lie of my parents that I bought into and that I repeated to myself daily and he offered me a new sentence. Now I was hearing, "We love who you are Laura, please show us more of you. We love you so much for who you are. God made you in such a beautiful way." Then in time, they encouraged me to believe it within myself. Praise God!

These Christians were messengers of God's love because they had his love in them to give out. They too walked in his love because for them, and me, it's who we are. Want to meet these wonderful people full of God's love? Then keep reading because they're at the next church.

Chapter 37

"Forget the former things; do not dwell on the past. See, I am doing a new thing! Now it springs up; do you not perceive it? I am making a way in the wilderness and streams in the wasteland." Isaiah 43:18-19NIV

SOMEONE ASKED ME if I regret everything I did and the hurt I caused. Kind of a no-brainer question really. What am I going to say? Yes, I enjoyed destroying relationships?

When you arrive in a place in your life where you've come through extreme trauma, and then you begin to look back and see so much hurt and pain you caused because of it, how could I not have regret!

Yet, we cannot allow ourselves to live in regret. We cannot allow ourselves to dwell on the past, the good or the bad. The last week I was in New Orleans my small group leader's wife took me into the woman's washroom at the church and berated me for ten solid minutes, venting on me all the frustration and anger she had towards me. She really let me have it non-stop because I had damaged them so much and hurt so many. It was her last chance to see me, and she wasn't going to let the opportunity go by. She was going to tell me exactly what she thought of me.

My life is full of regrets and hurt people. I destroyed so many budding friendships, and yet, today, I cannot dwell on that. I nearly destroyed my friendship with two of my closest friends in the fall of 2016.

Had it not been for God's love in them already, it would have been over. But they don't need me to be perfect for them. They just want me to be free of the pain, not for their benefit but for mine. That's God's love in them!

I know they both have rejoiced in all that God has done for me over the past few months and I know that they are so ready to exchange the memory of all the pain I caused them to celebrate with me, arm in arm, what God has done for me and the place of freedom I now stand. The love they showed me wasn't their own but his. Yet, God is working in me as well.

One said to me that it's so easy to forgive me because I'm always so fast to realize my sin against her and seek her forgiveness. I guess for me, I know what pain is like to receive, so when I know I have caused others pain, I seek them quickly to hopefully alleviate the damage and to let them know my regret. Do I regret much? Yes but I have exchanged my regret for a desire to do better.

We cannot change the past, but if we walk in obedience and humility today, it will be a good day, then the next and the next. Then in time, your recent days will become your recent past, full of positives and light, as you chose in previous days to honour God. How you do that is personal to each person. I know my friends are far happier that I'm not living in regret but living in his peace and hope!

Regret is such a sinkhole. Like fear, unbridled it can cause a lot of damage. Regret should spur us on to seek victory in Christ, not lead us to surrender and defeat!

Chapter 38

IN 2007 HE said to me, "I don't want you 'doing,' I want you 'willing'." Doing means my fleshly plans, what I think is the best way to serve him. Willing means to wait on him for his plans and for what he wants for me. We must be willing because sometimes God needs us to sit out a season, just as much as he needs us to step up in another. If we are willing, he can use us. When we're busy 'doing' for him, it may not be what he wants for us to at all.

Understand that willingness starts with humility, which stems from a healthy fear and respect of our Papa. For myself, since 2007, it has grown into a loving, gentle and caring relationship between myself and our Lord. He asks, and I am ready and willing to listen and do as he leads me. It's to say, I surrender Lord because as long as you know the plans you have for me, I don't need to know, and I trust you to lead me in all areas; including the dangerous ones. All of what he wrote me that night in 2007 was now coming to pass in my heart.

I wrote about my encounter with God that day in the car, where he gave me his love, but he had been showing me his love in others for a long time. Preparing me, so on that day, he could place it in me as well. He showed me his love in others, but I had no clue at what I was looking at because I didn't have his love in me yet. I had no frame of reference to know what it felt like, or looked like to have his love 'in you' and not just 'for you.'

Here are three examples from my time in New Orleans at the last church that I promised you earlier, that speak to that and profoundly changed my understanding of love.

Chapter 39

"As I live well, ride the waves of human emotion and dance to the rhythm of life, I can be swept away by the power and glory of the nature of God." - *Shelby Tobler Pruitt*

I USED TO WORK on the greeting team at the last church I attended in New Orleans. But one Sunday I ended up working the info desk alone. The great thing about the info desk is that it's in an alcove off the lobby. So, I was in the lobby, but it afforded me a view of all that was happening.

That Sunday I witnessed God's love working through one woman. I suspect that no one had ever seen it, but it took me being removed somewhat and more of an observer to see her walking out his love. This church had over 1000 in its one service on Sunday, and yet she knew everyone. I watched her hug so many, and ask them by name, how they were, then she waiting for a reply. She went from one person to the next, walking in such love and care that in no time the lobby permeated in God's love to the point that when unsaved visitors attended a service, they commented that they felt love in the lobby. That was her!

Her obedience and willingness to be used by him was making a huge difference. That lobby was his, and she was his hands and feet.

I remember writing a testimonial as to what I witnessed that day, and I shared it with the pastors, praising God for her because it was such a beautiful thing to see.

I also had the pleasure of knowing her in my small group. She was a very humble and caring person, seeking God every day. She also was so hospitable and held many gatherings in her home. What a joy she was to know! At Christmas, she gave me a twenty-five dollar gift certificate to a kitchen store. With it, I bought one of those metal food scrapers to gather up chopped items. Even today, I used it, and every time I look at it, it reminds me of a loving person that not only made the lobby of that church permeate in his love, but it reminded me of her selflessness and love she gave to me as well.

There was also another woman that I came to know. When I knew her, she was in a wheelchair with advancing ALS. I heard so many stories of her love for the young people that knew her kids. To all of them, she was like a second mom. She loved them all with his love and cared deeply for them. She truly was God's blessing to so many, yet, when I knew her the ravages of her disease were making her life difficult. There was one Sunday when it was clear that her body was failing her and that standing was not an option for her any longer.

During the worship service, I watched her force herself to her feet with all her might, then raise her hands over her head for a time, praising God with all she had. She stood among us and yet her worship was a thousand times more powerful, because for me in that moment, that one act of worship showed me what true love for him expressed looks like. It was a love that I had never seen before. Yes, I was close to him but not like that. She eventually sat again, and you could tell she was completely drained. In that one moment, it was as if she stood in his presence in every sense of the word, and left me wanting that kind of loving passion for him in my walk and in my worship.

She's gone to be with the Lord now and she never even knew me, yet I knew her and learned so much about his love through her.

A few months later, in the spring of 2011, I was leaving New Orleans to return to Canada when an older couple from church came to give me a sizable amount of money to help recover my car from the mechanic. Then, seeing that my moving help hadn't come, they immediately pitched in and helped pack my truck. After three hours of serving with love and energy in the hot New Orleans heat and humidity, the wife came to me so humble she could have been on her knees with the tone and words she used. She said to me that day, as she stared me in the eyes with such love and genuine care, "Thank you for the honor of serving you."

I was stunned when she said it to me. Never in my life had someone slaved for me for three hours on a hot sticky NOLA day and then humbly thanked me for the privilege! I remember leaving New Orleans that day but with a lot to ponder. I had no idea that kind of love even existed! That sentence propelled me onto a road to know his love first-hand.

For many weeks that sentence never left me. Yet, throughout all that time I just kept asking him for it. I wanted to humbly and lovingly say that sentence to another, and as the years passed, I began to crave it!

The next chapter is a piece I wrote in 2015 about just this.

Chapter 40

From the piece, I wrote in 2015.

The Morning My Life Changed

IN THE SUMMER, I began to attend a new church. It's a place where Jesus is truly walked out, and genuine love is all that I have seen from everyone. I was also surrounded by so many places to serve. Yet, I knew I was to stay still and wait on the Lord as to where to plug in.

I had been praying to God for the opportunity to serve and where to serve, throughout the summer. I kept saying to him, "Wherever I serve you, Lord, I don't want any fanfare, I don't want any glory or recognition, I just want to serve quietly – washing dishes is good with me, I will do anything, and I will thank you for the chance and thank them for the honour of serving them."

Then ten days ago, I set out from my home at 6:30 am Sunday morning to work in the kitchen in a homeless/near homeless outreach center called Regeneration.

Regen (for short) does more than serve breakfast 365 days a year to those in this once small town of 36,000 where I was born, that now touts a population of over 500,000 residents. They provide clothes and personal care items, showers, laundry, medical services and so many other tangibles. Yet, the one thing they offer most of all is love that comes from the amazing staff.

I know one personally, and she is such a loving sister in the Lord. I am so honoured to call her a friend. For her, as the volunteer coordinator to come to this special place every day is such a joy for her. Her face lights up when she talks about it as the joy just flows from her. Sure, she can complain at times about scheduling issues - we all can, but 10 minutes later she is glowing with praises to God that she loves her job so very much and loves those who God has blessed her to know and help. For a brief moment ten days ago I was able to share in her joy.

In the dark pre-dawn fall morning I messed up on the address, and I was a bit late coming in, but I did make it. With help, I found the kitchen, and when I arrived, it was already in full swing as many guests waited at the tables for breakfast. I met the head of the kitchen. A lovely woman named Carol but in that moment, she seemed to me more like a top-kick boot camp sergeant and that kitchen was her battlefield. She told me to wash my hands, (A precursor to my day as I would come to discover.) get a hair net and put on an apron.

She had me fetch a few times and then had me prep the water in the large sinks. I said to her that I am an excellent cook, I've taught cooking classes and that I could help chop or prep.

"Nope, you prep the water."

I told her that I had no idea what she wanted. She grimaced at me like I had called her away from the battle plans for the invasion of Normandy to help me, but she did come over.

"Soap water here, rinse water here with bleach." She then turned and walked away again – back to the invasion plans or perhaps prepping the ham.

One of the regular volunteers looked at my kind of lost expression and said, "Don't worry, you'll be busy soon."

Then it suddenly dawned on me that I was the dishwasher. And at that moment I broke out laughing. I mean laughing my guts out, so everyone looked at me laughing. I asked God to be a lowly dish washer months earlier and that I would be honoured to be that. Now, here I was standing in the kitchen of a shelter appointed for this shift to be the dish washer. God came through for me, and my smile was so real and so humble. Suddenly, I didn't want to chop veggies, I knew I was where I belonged.

We had a few more come in and start to help with the many tasks, but soon the dishes started to pile up, and I was washing them like a pro. Wash, rinse and place in the plastic bins. Then the regular showed me the dish cooker. It's this big stainless steel box, with gauges, lights and buttons. It looked like a robot in a 60's 'B' rated Sci-Fi movie. Kind of like, Robbie the robot meets Mr Clean but with two levers like a slot machine on each side.

So, my regular, (I come to find out serves every weekend,) drags my champion cleaned and washed dishes into this box after pulling the lever. But, instead of wheels spinning and coins dropping, the box rises up to reveal some chrome spray nozzles. He slides the tray in and drops the handle as the box closes. Then I could hear, in that 'B' movie soundtrack – "It's alive!" The lights flashed, and the gauges went all over, and then it calmed down and stopped about a minute later. He pulls the lever and out pops ridiculously hot steaming dishes. You know the kind you mom tells you not to touch, haha, well, we touch them and oh yeah mom, they really are hot.

So, 90 minutes go by and I've been going non-stop. I look back at the food being served. Omelets with fresh peppers and onions, toast, croissants, fresh fruit, yogurt and good spiral ham, warmed by Carol with love and served with orange juice, smiles and care.

I announce to the air. "Whew, I need a break." And Sargent Carol says to me. "Yeah girl, go out there and take a break." So I head out into the eating area to find the guy with the Cowboy hat with a star on it, I saw getting his breakfast earlier. He goes by the name of Tex. I sit down with him and another older man who looked like Patrick Stewart - you know, Captain Picard of the Enterprise. Well, we start talking about this quaint little town we used to know that is now a mega city. Tex is an old man with gray hair and a scruffy beard but with a good heart. He reminded me of the bearded guy that was in all of the John Wayne westerns - he would drive the stage coach.

Well, it wasn't as dramatic as all that, but what I did come to find after some time spent with these two men was that I cared about them, I really cared about them! I eventually excused myself and prepared to go back to work, but before I did, I looked out over the people eating, and all I could see in everyone in this room were God's children, just like me. I cannot write what I felt in that moment, the tears flow, even now, recalling it but I was changed that day – really changed. I saw lost souls, beaten up hearts and struggling people trying to hold onto hope. Then I looked in the kitchen and my fellow co-workers, prepping and serving, meal after meal, and I felt so thankful to have the privilege to be one of them.

But like everything in life, breakfast ended, and I cleaned my last dish, put away my last plate and put the hair net back and left the apron in a pile to be laundered.

I did actually have the breakfast, it was better than I ate that morning at home. Perhaps even more special because the food, the gas for the stoves, the electricity, the heat, the equipment, and lights - everything was given to us to help these people know there is hope in this world.

I exited the basement and went to my car. It was light out as I began to drive to church when it all hit me. Like a storm it hit me, and I sobbed! Really sobbed!

The faces of those who we loved on, the care, the joy I was blessed to show them and receive - it hit me! I was so overwhelmed - so changed by it - so, different for it. I saw these people differently. I saw them like Jesus sees them - and me! I was given a gift this day. A gift to know what my friend who works there experiences every day of her life. I found the greatest joy I have ever known. The joy of loving on people, just like me and not once did I think of myself all morning!

Regeneration is truly a special place. A place God led me to. A place to see, find and embrace the heart of his son.

Please help keep the love going by giving to this amazing place! www.regenbrampton.com

Chapter 41

My Days in God's Soul Rehab

"It's time to locate the lies and the liars—and reject the labels they've created. I believe the voice of God is calling us out of our hiding with a question that at once exposes and embraces us: "Who told you that?"... The serpent gets nervous when we start challenging the doubts, dysfunctions and insecurities his questions have propagated in our lives. When we discover what God has really said, we experience a liberation that leads to fulfillment." Steven Furtick

I ARRIVE AT MY new church whose motto is, "A church for people who aren't into church." The church is called, 'The Meeting House.' They have a single building for services and broadcasts in Oakville, Ontario and then satellite locations, generally, movie theatres they rent, all over the area and beyond.

Each site had an overseeing pastor. But the real work of the church is in the 'home churches' as they're called. Those who lead these groups, in someone's home every week, are considered pastors to a small flock and are charged with the duty and responsibility to love and care for them. The first time I listened online, I listened to the teaching pastor by the name of Bruxy Cavey. I remember thinking, wow, he is all about God's love and nothing else. But it wasn't just him. I had come to a church where everyone I met had God's heart in them, and they all genuinely loved me.

I remember telling the site pastor my story, and he was like, 'Yeah, so, whatever, where would you like to serve?' He didn't care in the least because he saw me through the eyes of Christ and in turn, he simply saw a beautiful creation and a gift from God.

I remember telling one person that I have a congenital birth defect and she demanded that I never use that term again. She was very upset with me and said that there's nothing defective about me at all and God made me this way for a reason and that I was knitted together in my mom's womb and that I was fearfully and wonderfully made.

In fact, everyone demanded that I begin to love myself and to embrace who God made me to be, to stop believing a lie set in my brain as a tiny child that I was a mistake but to believe and know that God doesn't make mistakes. I was made this way so his power could be seen through me and that I'm beautiful.

For the first time in my life, Christians were helping me to begin to believe in myself, and they kept at me, over and over, reinforcing God's truth, God's love and God's heart for me into my soul, sharing his love for me and helping me overcome so much. They took on my burdens and walked with me, despite my volatile emotions at times, as I was still dealing with much automatic stuff in me. They were dedicated to helping God speak life into my soul.

Yet, there was one person who continually spoke against all they said to me. It was an endless knock on the gift of God's love that they were showing me. This person loathed me more than anyone I have ever encountered and told me repeatedly that I was of no use to anyone.

That person was me because that's all I had ever heard and then repeated to myself.

I loathed myself and hated myself so much my entire life. I loathed the way he made me and the way my parents forced me to be. I loathed everything about me. In time, I came to realize that this was the greatest hindrance in my life for finding the ultimate freedom I sought and needed. How can I love others as myself (Mark 12:31) when deep down I hate myself right down to the very core of who I am!

I now belonged to a church that taught about the love of Christ and seeing everything and interpreting everything through the lens of Christ. I was learning so much about having his heart. Here is a sentence from one of Bruxy's sermons that was so powerful I had to write it down:

"When we are touched by the grace of Christ, and we turn around and offer that grace to others; we can be a beautiful power for love and for light and for reconciliation in this world. Ultimately, between us and God and then with one another."

In time I began to realize that I was in God's soul rehab. I was being flooded with his love through so many, and I was healing from the inside out. Yet despite being free of the anger and bitterness, I was so damaged. Massive healing was needed. I needed him to show me who I really was in him, which they continually repeated to me. They spoke life and light into my dark and hopeless soul and helping me gain, for the first time in my life, self-worth and self-esteem. They were helping me rewrite what I said to myself that others had instilled in me. Helping me speak life over myself and not death.

To be honest, it was hard to hear. I heard their words but receiving them was not easy because the words of death were so ingrained in my soul.

It was their constant, unwavering support, speaking life into me at every opportunity that eventually won out, as I slowly began to replace the death words I spoke over myself with words of life. But most of all, they helped me to see that I was beautiful, loved and valued just the way I am; things I never heard anyone say about me before in my life.

For the first time in my life, I was openly and deeply loved just the way I am.

Chapter 42

A genuine reconciliation can only come when both parties are humbled before God in their heart and ready to love one another with genuine mercy. Anything else is an exercise in futility, designed to appease man and satisfy others. It will not last for it's only for outward appearances but not of the heart.

GOD GAVE ME that understanding above because part of me still hopes, for those who had hurt me so brutally, that they would seek me out and reconcile with me. I have nothing against them. Yes, I had been deeply hurt and couldn't understand why they chose to keep kicking me when I was so very clearly down and defenseless. I certainly wanted them to see that I was being honest about myself and that they were just incorrect. Yet, that would take the work of the Holy Spirit. Here is a nugget of truth he gave me long ago that is so accurate:

"It's not your job to change the hearts and minds of people; that's my job. Your job is to do my will and leave the rest to me."

He helped me see, that if change was to occur in their hearts regarding me, it would be strictly his doing. I hold out hope that one day, someone who was party to the sinful actions perpetrated against me, will come to see that they were dreadfully wrong. That they would realize that what they did was horribly sinful and hurtful, and as a result, would feel convicted and seek me out to set things right with me.

It hasn't happened yet, but I have hope.

Throughout my experience of being abused by Christians, there have always been supporters of mine who have said to me as I was being abused, "Now you know how Christ felt." Because they knew that, like Jesus, I had done nothing to warrant the abuse.

Yet, I'm sure Jesus would have preferred that the religious types had put down their pride and followed him instead of trying to discredit and destroy him and in the end plot his death.

It's good to know I'm walking in his footsteps in knowing the injustice of being unfairly accused. However, to be honest, it wasn't this part that I wanted to embrace. What I asked God to help me do was respond to my persecutors as he did; with love. It was his heart for those who were persecuting him that I wanted. It was never about my vindication. I sought him to help me love these people as he loves.

"If you love only those who love you, what reward is there in that? Even corrupt tax collectors do that much" Matthew 5:46 NLT

"The true indicator of a Christian's heart is when they honour people who have nothing to give back." - Steven Furtick

Chapter 43

BY THE SPRING of 2016, I knew my time at the Meeting House, was short. I had managed to ruin my relationship with several, but unfortunately, it was the site pastor and his wife most of all. Despite God working on me, I still had issues and automatic responses, still unidentified and therefore unresolved that caused such destruction in others, and as a result, I was being shut out of this church, and in time it was clear that the pastor wasn't going to allow me to serve.

It wasn't him. I was just so up and down, and I didn't know why. Unsteady was the best word to describe me. Even the best of us cannot just forget the damage done and hurts perpetrated by others. I knew the site pastor possessed the heart of Christ, and that he forgave me, and yet because I was so unsteady he required much time to pass before he could get past my actions against him, and in turn, watch to see if I was ready to be released to serve. But this was moot really because he had no contact with me and there was no one in authority to let him know how I was doing.

By July I was led by the Lord to attend a different church for the rest of the summer. During my first service, I sat on the aisle in the back row right near the entrance.

As the worship began, I stood for a time but ended up sitting. By the second song, the usher behind me began to praise God under her breath. She was pacing all over the place behind me, speaking praises to him and she was getting louder and louder as the Holy Spirit moved her. Then, as the music died down into the instrumental, she began to shout into the back of my head, "I speak against the spirit of destruction that is upon you!" She said more, but all the other words surrounded this central sentence.

When she finished, she touched my shoulder, and I suddenly realized that she was speaking this over me, and touched me for a brief moment so I would know that it was for me specifically and not a prophetic proclamation to the church. After I got home, I ran online to find what the spirit of destruction is. In time, I found this description. See if this doesn't EXACTLY match my life history:

"A destructive spirit is one that ultimately wants to destroy a person to the core and kill them. The meaning of the word destroy is 'to reduce something to useless fragments or a useless form or to injure beyond repair' according to Webster's college dictionary. It also means to put an end to or demolish. In essence, it's a spirit that has come to reduce a person's livelihood into a uselessness and then put an end to them."

This revelation was so powerful because when we know what the enemy is up to with us, we can defend against his schemes. Knowledge is victory because once we know what he's trying to pull, we don't fall for it any longer. I suspect that had God given Adam and Eve a do-over, the serpent would not have been successful with more apples.

The enemy had been trying to destroy me before I could ever talk and had used so many 'loving Christians' to try to shut me down. To get me to hide away and die. To leave church never to return. To keep silent. Certainly to never write a book and share my story so his power and glory could be seen. The enemy was after my destruction, and unwittingly so many in our tribe had helped him with great determination and pride. I finally understood his scheme for me, and in that understanding, he became powerless.

It was also part one of three that God used so he could finally help me come home to freedom.

Chapter 44

IN SEPTEMBER, I formally left the Meeting House because God was leading me to move on. I cannot say enough wonderful things about them. They were there for me when I needed God's words of life in soul rehab. I needed unconditional love, and they gave that to me. They loved me even more because of my condition, not in spite of it. They showed me his love for me through much grace. Every time I thought I had hurt someone to the point that they would send me packing, they would seek to love me in return!

"There is no greater love than to lay down one's life for one's friends."
John 15:13 NLT

It seemed that everyone was walking that out with me, all cheering me on to wholeness and walking beside me, as God healed me of so much. I wasn't angry any longer, but I was still struggling emotionally in so many ways. 'A church for people who aren't into church.' Interesting tag line. Many who go to the Meeting House have been abused by 'loving Christians' and yet possess his love.

I said earlier that one of the ways to gain his love in us is through hardship. It comes when we choose to never do to others what others have done to us, and we seek him for a better way to live and to gain his heart. It's the day we say, "I surrender Lord, live in me 100% and show me your love."

James 4:10 says that when we humble ourselves to him, he will lift us up. It's strictly the work of the spirit that gives us his heart, filled with his love and grace within us.

I am so thankful to these folks, as God led me to the church I presently attend. I am still very much welcome at the Meeting House, and I care a great deal about so many there and still see them on occasion.

In fact, my book launch for this book will take place at the same Meeting House Pastor's home. He and his wife are such a gift to me as my acknowledgement of them at the beginning of the book attests to.

Chapter 45

IN SEPTEMBER, at my new church, I joined a small group and attended my first gathering. Yet, before our second time together, the leader of the group, at the prompting of the Holy Spirit, asked me to write a devotional and gave me just thirty-six hours to write it and be prepared to share.

I prayed for a time but knew the devotional had to be about what he had been showing me for a few months. Below is the devotional I wrote.

But even more important for my journey to freedom, by prompting the leader to ask me, it forced me to write down all that he was showing me, ponder it further and then organize it into a logical document that I shared that night, which I share now. It was also part two of three of my freedom.

As far as I'm concerned, it's the most powerful document I've ever written because it came from him. I'm glad you have the chance to read it as well.

Tonight's devotional is about perceptions.

We all deal with perceptions the same way. We perceive something. We then interpret what we see. Then we assume things, and then we judge.

""Go, find out where he is," the king ordered, "so I can send men and capture him." The report came back: "He is in Dothan." Then he sent horses and chariots and a strong force there. They went by night and

surrounded the city. When the servant of the man of God got up and went out early the next morning, an army with horses and chariots had surrounded the city. "Oh no, my lord! What shall we do?" the servant asked. "Don't be afraid," the prophet answered. "Those who are with us are more than those who are with them." And Elisha prayed, "Open his eyes, Lord, so that he may see." Then the Lord opened the servant's eyes, and he looked and saw the hills full of horses and chariots of fire all around Elisha." 2 King 6:13-17 NIV

The servant must have thought 'all is lost.' He looked for an action plan in his emotional state. He saw an entire army, and he wanted a solution fast. He was in a complete state of fear driven panic. He perceived the army. He interpreted this as a threat. He assumed they would attack and kill everyone and he judged that it was time to flee. In this case, the servant was panicking for nothing. All wasn't lost, everything was just fine.

Notice that Elisha didn't answer his question at all. What he did instead, was give his servant more information which began to change his perception. Then Elisha asked God to show his servant the whole story, the whole truth that the servant's perception didn't offer—a heavenly army surrounding the physical one. The servant was ready to act. He saw the army, his perception was accurate and yet he judged wrong because he didn't know all the facts.

"As they sailed, he fell asleep. A squall came down on the lake, so that the boat was being swamped and they were in great danger. The disciples went and woke him, saying, "Master, Master, we're going to drown!" He got up and rebuked the wind and the raging waters; the storm subsided and all was calm. "Where is your faith?" he asked his disciples." Luke 8 23-25a NIV

Here the disciples perceived raging waves swamping their boat. They interpreted it as a real danger to their lives because as seasoned fisherman they knew when a storm could kill. They assumed that without everyone working together they would perish and they judged Jesus as uncaring because he slept instead of helping bail. Despite their perception being accurate, it wasn't accurate because they didn't have the whole story. How often are we ready to abandon our faith when we perceive the worst?

How amazing this story would have been had they looked at Jesus sleeping in the back of the boat and perceived that there was no danger and slept with him. Because, despite the waves, Jesus slept, so they had nothing to fear. Yet what did Jesus say to them in the end? Where is your faith?

Perceptions are truly of the devil because they're highly deceptive. No matter how accurate they appear to be, they aren't. They are actually inherently inaccurate, woefully incomplete and lacking of full understanding. I'm not speaking about God breathed perceptions but those of our own design. Included in our design is this: "Well it's something I know God would want me to do." That is on us, not him, make no mistake.

So let's unpack how we go from perceiving something to acting upon it. Note that nearly always, acted upon perceptions leads to hurt, pain and destruction.

First is the interpretation.

When we perceive things not only are they incomplete of facts, we usually interpret it through our filter of past emotional baggage, which will distort things even further by how we interpret what we perceive. A poor interpretation can radically dial-up what we ultimately do or say as it always feeds off our emotions.

Next is assumptions.

Assuming is going from perceived facts to conjecture, guessing or making reasonable conclusions without facts.

To assume is to believe something to be true without any evidence that it is. There's a legal objection for it in court. 'Assuming fact's not in evidence.' How often do we assume things regarding others based on our perceptions and not facts?

For example, we need to ask ourselves, 'Did they actually say, what I assume they are thinking about me?' Why is it easier for us to assume the worst about someone and not the best? Doesn't gossip usually start here?

Lastly, after we assume 'facts that are not in evidence,' and dialed up emotionally by our own personal history, the perception becomes fact, so factual that we can then pass judgment on others. Yet the Bible says:

"Who are you to judge someone else's servant? To their own master, servants stand or fall. And they will stand, for the Lord is able to make them stand." Romans 14:4 NIV

Sometimes we judge a situation, like Elisha's servant did, but we saw how wrong he was.

Sometimes we say, "I'm giving them the benefit of the doubt." But that's just making a postponed judgment. But why are we judging anyone at all?

Jesus spoke about judging someone with the twig in their eye while we have the log in ours. The Bible says to leave the judging to God because God sees the heart, man only judges the outward. How can we judge others when that statement itself says we don't have all the facts? Ultimately, perceptions so easily drive our heart, attitude, behaviour and our actions. I've touched on the mechanics of perceptions but here is a list of what acted upon perception looks like after we interpret them, assume things and judge.

Perceptions breed fear, violence, drama, misunderstandings, a lack of peace, worry, discontentment, war, hate, self-righteousness, revenge, anger, distrust, gossip, unfounded accusations, disunity, impatience, pride, arrogance and the destruction of relationships.

So what do we do?

First, note that perceptions aren't accurate. We can choose to ignore what we see, but that takes faith, something that Jesus said we need. We should choose not to let our emotional baggage interpret things. This is very difficult because where emotions and past hurts are involved, humans tend to 'act' and 'react' by emotional instinct, not faith. We must overcome this issue and not allow our instinct to rule our thoughts and actions. Unfortunately, it's also the most difficult thing to do. It's where I fall most often.

We must stop making assumptions. We need to say to ourselves, "Facts not in evidence," when assuming thoughts plague our mind. We need to recognize the lies for what they are.

Lastly, we need to recognize that only God knows all the facts. Note that Elisha's servant was shown by God himself the complete and accurate truth. And the disciples were shown by Jesus that they were panicking in that boat for nothing. God is the only one who knows the complete story and can give us the complete story. Even those intimately involved in something rarely have all the facts. There's a saying by gossipers, "perception is everything." Actually, perception is meaningless; it's faith in God that's everything.

If we are to beat this, we need to invite others into our struggle and seek objective godly counsel, especially if we find that our baggage is really messing with us and pushing us to sin. But more than that, we need to pray and seek God for his peace and that he would guide us and help us submit to his will.

"Trust in the Lord with all your heart and lean not on your own understanding; in all your ways submit to him and he will make your paths straight. Do not be wise in your own eyes." Proverbs 3:5-7a NIV

Chapter 46

My Homecoming!

"Even if they are judging you, being controlled by the opinions of others is a sure way to miss all the unique plans God has for your future." Sue Augustine

I WROTE THAT devotional and began to see clearly in my life how perceptions were the ruin of me. Not only was I the victim of them but I was using false perceptions to perpetrate such sin on those who entered my life solely to love me.

This devotional had helped me, and it got me near the finish line, but I was still missing something. I didn't understand relationships well enough to correct what I was doing. I needed a guide to help me understand clearly what I was specifically doing that was causing heartache and trouble so I could stop doing it.

Then, quite by chance, I found and watched a video series called "Girlfriend Revolution" with Susan Thomas, and I finally found the last pieces to my struggle. I can't even begin to share this teaching with you. It would be criminal to try to take out of context all the amazing and life altering relational things I discovered about myself through this series.

This series was part three of three of my freedom, and it took me from being a destroyer of friendships to being a valued, loving, generous and caring friend virtually overnight. Not only to those who respond in friendship but to all in my life because I had no more issues getting in the way. I was finally able to use the heart of love he gave me, to love and serve those in my life no matter who they are.

I learned through her course that if I'm looking for something in response in a friendship, then my motive isn't right. God sometimes designs us to have one-way friendships. The whole time with them it's to serve them and love them and not ever get anything in return. It's knowing that my reward and strength to love this person comes from Jesus and not this person. It's to treat all those in our lives as gifts from God.

Think about that in your own life. Would you still be the dedicated and devoted friend you are with those in your life if it only went one way and they never gave back to you? It's a huge motivation tester.

I strongly encourage you to get her DVDs. No other video series and I've seen dozens, has ever spoken to me more deeply than this one!

http://www.girlfriendrevolution.com/

For me, I discovered that I was in friendships to gain time with them. I would even lavish gifts on these people to be near them longer. I was so alone that I would do anything and manipulate them to get more time with them.

She showed me that ultimately Jesus can only be our source for our needs. If we are looking to others for what only he can provide, we will demand of others and burn them out. Jesus must be the sole source of all in our life, and we must solidify and strengthen our relationship with him first before we go near others or we will detrimentally seek from them what only Jesus can give us.

The second thing that I came to discover is that I'm an extremely sensitive person by nature. I take everything said to me to heart. However, when you add a hyper sensitive personality, then add in years of abuse and conditioning that makes me believe the worst of everyone, then add what I perceive to be an offense - real or imagined, and just watch those play on each other. And as Susan puts it, "Watch the crazy lady thinking comes out." As I began to react out of fear, my sensitivity and perception began to play on each other. Oh, what massive damage I caused to so many because of this! That part of her message, along with so many other things, helped me finally understand myself and the mechanics and pitfalls that destroyed my relationships with others.

At one point she said, 'okay here is a pitfall we can have in our relationship...' and then went on to describe me! Sadly, she did that so many times describing me with different issues it was depressing! I was seeking and demanding of others for what only God could give me, and I was allowing my perceptions and baggage and my hyper sensitive nature to make me believe all kinds of things that were untrue. This was the most important discovery of my life, and yet irreparable damage had already been done to so many.

A few weeks after this revelation and the freedom I found myself in, as a result, God wrote me a letter and shared with me his heart for me moving forward.

At the time, I was deeply lamenting the loss of two of my closest friends from the Meeting House because of the things I had done to them. They had stood by me for so long, but they both had reached their limit on how many times they would allow me to bully, demand, manipulate, falsely accuse and hurt them before they needed to step back from me.

I was now finally past hurting others as I had in my past, and yet, I deeply lamented that these two very caring women, who I cherished so much, would be the last casualties of that hurt and desperate person I once was.

Earlier I shared with you the first letter God wrote me. Now, here is his last letter to me, to date, regarding my loss of them at the time. It was written to me, but I know we can all benefit from it.

Hear the huge tone change in his words to me now. Feel and embrace the depth of his love. Not a stern disciplinarian as before in 2007 but now the profoundly loving friend and Saviour we worship.

My dearest Laura, I love you so much. How you struggle to know and believe me in your life! I have shown you my loving hand, and somehow you expect hurt instead of love. This is about your faith in me now. Do you have sufficient faith in me to trust me no matter how dire things look? Let go Laura. Let go! This is not a time to lament loss but celebrate the green pastures I have led you into. Resting in me means just that! Trust, faith hope and peace in it all.

You have cried out to me. I have heard your cries. But know that I know what's best for you, not just in this time but in all times. Let go Laura. Rest in me and do it. Dance and be of great joy. You asked to know me more. Then do these things not in your own futile strength but in my unending and powerful strength. The key to joy is spending time with me. It's a lesson I shared with you a long time ago that you needed reminding of.

I am your shepherd, you do have all that you need. [PS:23]You leave others to me. This is a time of separation for you all. Leave it to me and rest. They too have lessons to learn in me before you reunite. Best to come together in unity under me, then out of duty. I can heal anything my dear daughter but for tonight and for your future, stop lamenting and start praising me. This is the heart I want you to have. Praising people are positive people.

It's up to you. You cried out to me and I gave you an answer, the rest is up to you. Praise me or lament your loss. Be positive and a joy to know, or lament your losses and be a drag to know. [Praise me,] Not by your circumstances but by me, find your joy and smile. Be at peace daughter. Cry out to me in praise and joy, make this your soul and you will truly find genuine peace.

As I wrote, I cannot walk in regret. That won't bring my friends back. It's walking in the freedom he has given me and being the lover of others that I now am in my heart and life. I knew that to truly love them meant that I had to give them their freedom from me, no strings attached.

I had to seek Jesus as my number one relationship and get my needs met through him. I had to let them go, and let Jesus show me the riches he has for me first, then walk out his love for others from my joy-filled and complete heart.

Today I can report that after a few months I'm honoured that they, once again, call me a friend and that they both have completely forgiven me!

They forgave me because I began to look forward as I choose every day to be the loving person he has finally made me be. That's what they see and hear and know about me and why they came back.

Always willing, always trying to improve and follow him, every day; closer and closer. Giving people grace, being ready to forgive before an offense has occurred, being willing to obey God without question or argument. Desperate at all time for the opportunity to lovingly serve others so I can thank them for the honour.

That's what our Christian walk is all about Charlie Brown.

He has blessed me with a peace I have never known, even in the trials I've faced since my homecoming. I have faith and love. But beyond that, God has given me joy! Joy in him and a joy to share. A joy to bring love and light and hope to those I encounter, and most of all, joy to those who live in the grey zone but don't know him yet.

Praising people truly ARE positive people.

Conclusion

MY ONLY complaint about the Christmas Carol is that when Scrooge finally gets set free, that part of the story is so short! It needs to be three times longer!

I'd love to go on and on about my homecoming and the joy I now feel, but it's only been a few months. I suppose the greatest thing that came from my freedom is the book you are now holding. I watched Girlfriend Revolution in late October, and two months later God prompted me to begin this book. The first draft was 80% written in just one week between Christmas and New Years in 2016.

Many at the Meeting House who heard my story told me to write it, and yet, I sensed that it wasn't time, and I was right. I needed to be set free, and be in the place of victory and peace in him to give you an ending.

My automatic, negative and destructive actions and reaction were in the way of the love he put in me that day in my car, and in the end, I found that I was getting in the way of him using me. He ultimately got me out of the way and set me free so he could set you free!

I am so thankful to God for everything in my life! Today, I am slowly making good friendships and relationships born out of a desire to serve and love, not take and demand. And that crazy lady thinking? Yeah, she left town for good, because I now accept people for who they are and cherish them as gifts from God.

Even one of my pastors, not knowing any of what changed for me, recently commented that he has seen a huge change in me since the summer of 2016. I will praise God forever for that comment because it means that others are seeing the power of God's work being accomplished in me!

Also, I knew that I would be a devotional speaker one day, although at the time he told me a few years ago, I was stumped as to how he was going to pull that off. Then he tells me that my next book, after writing my novel, would be a book about love. I was equally stumped as to how I could possibly write a book like that, and yet, you just read it!

So how do I conclude all that you've read?

Perhaps the better question is how do you conclude all that you've read?

For me, this book ultimately is about God's love that we can seek him to have in us.

I find that when we all try to walk that out, regardless of how successful we are, or where we are in our faith journey, we all become part of a wonderful stained glass window where each of us is a beautiful and uniquely coloured and shaped pieces of glass. The light is the same source; it's the Holy Spirit in us.

What binds the glass together in an actual stained glass window is lead. But, for us, it's his love in us all, binding us all together in perfect unity. It's in that place that we can truly appreciate the God of the universe and shed his wonderful and colourful light onto this drab world that so desperately needs his love.

Imagine our church, the Church of Christ, walking in his absolute love and seeing everyone through his loving eyes. Imagine how many would come to him if we put down our will and broke down the walls that divide our planet and all humbly seek to become as Christ, for each other and for the lost.

When we allow God be God in our life and heart, imagine the new vistas and new things we could see so that one day he may touch us and put his love in us all, to be united under Christ. That we might reach out and embrace every last person in the world with his unconditional love and lead them home to himself.

The definition of encourage is to instill courage in the person, to believe again what is possible. To inspire someone is to take a person beyond what they thought possible and to believe attainable, what was once considered impossible.

I hope that through our journey together, God used my story to meet you where you are, encourage you and hopefully inspire you as well!

Shalom

.

This is a short story I wrote in 2015. God had led me to write Rachael's Quest beginning in 2010, and I did. But then, one day, I was reading Luke 7 about the unnamed woman who doted at Jesus' feet.

God suddenly told me to write her story and give her a name. I said to him that it's obvious from the text that she was a follower based on her devotion to him. Am I to write what it feels like to have an encounter with the Holy Spirit as we come to Christ in salvation?

God responded yes.

So, this is her story and what Jesus did for her as best as I could ever hope to write it. You will note that she too lived in the grey zone, cast there as a young woman and yet Jesus loved her regardless.

When Jesus said he hung around with sick people in need of a doctor, what he meant was that the one thing we all need and especially for those living in the grey zone is love. God's love, pure and real.

The words Jesus speaks at the end of the story are directly out of the NLT Bible. I didn't alter them at all. I just put a narrative around them.

Enjoy.

The Encounter (from Luke7:34-50 NLT)

Chapter 1

TAMAR WOKE early in the morning and grimaced, as she moved to sit at the end of her bed. He had left earlier in the night after he was 'done' with her. Yet, despite her self-imposed rule about staying awake should a client come, Tamar had fallen asleep. She cursed herself for spending precious time sleeping instead of working. Still, for Tamar, it was getting harder and harder for her to keep up the pace she had set for herself.

She gently rubbed her eyes with her palms. 'All the men.' 'All those men!' she thought. Some were new, some were married, and some single but most were regulars. Yet, they all had one thing in common—they all had money to spend on Tamar, the harlot.

Tamar heard a mother and her daughter on the street below and began to remember her time at home as a small girl. She remembered how her mother would call her 'my little sweet one'since her name meant 'date' like the kind you eat. Tamar never felt like that. Even at an early age, she always felt small and unworthy to be the niece of a Hebrew judge. Her uncle was kind enough, but his affection wasn't directed at Tamar or her mother. He had taken them both in when Tamar was a baby as a kinsmen redeemer, and although he did his duty and did what was right in the eyes of the law, Tamar had no love.

At thirteen, Tamar was caught with an older boy, and despite her mother pleading for mercy for her daughter, her brother's pride and reputation as a Hebrew judge was threatened, so he immediately removed Tamar from his home to live on the streets as an outcast, never to see her mother or uncle again.

Tamar slipped on her robe and moved to the slatted coverings on the window and opened them to reveal the street below. She peered down while remaining in the shadows. She kept a low profile during the early time of the day when the normal women were out since they would verbally attack her nearly as badly as the priests.

She sighed as she stared at the wealthy women, as well as the modest seeking provisions for their family. The fish monger, baker butcher and many other merchants lined the street to wait on them. These were normal women with husbands and children and families. Women who were whole and complete and knew real love.

Tamar looked around her room in contrast and choked back her tears. She felt so empty and used. She had nothing to show for her life and no chance to be normal. She would forever be shunned—she was Tamar, the harlot.

Eventually, she turned and sat at the side of her bed and looked at the coins he had left her a few hours earlier. He had always been generous with her but last night was exceptional. She stared at the seven gold aureus, yet she couldn't bring herself to pick them up or even look at them a moment longer. She looked down at her hands that trembled. She tried to will them to stop as she balled them up, but the trembling never ceased. She looked up and stared at the coins once more and knew in that moment she couldn't do this work anymore. The tears began to roll down her cheeks as she closed her eyes. Tamar wanted desperately to pray to Yahweh, but she remembered, as she was forced to leave her home, her uncle screaming not to bother praying to Yahweh because he doesn't forgive adulterers and that she was forever separated from him with no hope. That day, she was labelled a sinner and within a few days the people she had known from an early age, suddenly weren't speaking to her. Some even spat on her. Whatever it took to separate themselves from her, so the priests always nearby, always watching and listening, would see their purity.

Despite what her uncle said, Tamar slipped off her bed to her knees and began to pray.

Chapter 2

THAT EVENING, Tamar and her friend Argyros, a Greek tax collector, sat eating at a local street vendor selling roasted lamb, bread and vegetables. Argyros had grown accustomed to lively and exciting talks about many subjects with Tamar, but this evening Tamar sat and ate, saying little. Finally, Argyros leaned into her and whispered, "Why so down tonight, my friend?"

Tamar shrugged and smiled slightly. "I don't know, I guess I just wish I had another life."

"Ha!" Argyros shouted loudly. "So do we all, my friend!"

Tamar looked away to hide her face. Then brought her hand up to her eyes and wiped them.

Argyros softened his gaze. "My friend, why do you weep?"

Tamar shook her head.

"What is it, Tamar?" Argyros repeated so gently to her.

Eventually, Tamar turned to him and stared into his eyes. "Why do you like me?"

Argyros was perplexed. "What do you mean? This –'Why do you like me?'"

Tamar pleaded. "Just what I asked you. Why do you like me?"

Argyros stared at his friend's tortured face and sighed as he responded. "I like you because you like Argyros. You don't judge me for the job I do. You make me laugh! I love it when you sing and dance a happy dance after you drink too much wine." Argyros laughed. "You have a good laugh, and you make Argyros smile. You are a good friend, Tamar and you care. That is why Argyros likes you."

Tamar stared at him for a moment. "Argyros, if I ask you a question can you answer?"

He grinned. "You ask Argyros the quantity of wine before it's pressed but go ahead."

"Do you think Yahweh is real?"

Argyros grimaced. "Your Hebrew god? I do not know, Tamar. Go ask your priests, see if they know."

Tamar shook her head slowly. "I can't."

"Yes, Argyros understands. To them you are scum." Argyros spat on the ground defiantly. "That is what I think of them."

Tamar stared at his angry expression but her tears only increased.

Argyros softened his expression once more and quietly spoke. "Tamar, I have heard of a man who might be able to help you."

"Who is this man?"

"I heard about him from a traveler. This Hebrew man heals the sick and knows much. I also heard that he openly defies the priests. If there was anyone who could answer your question it would be him."

Tamar turned her head and stared into the distance deep in thought for a time, then turned back to her friend. "Where is this man?"

"Argyros does not know for sure, my friend but I heard he may be nearby."

Tamar reached over and kissed his cheek.

"Oh!" Argyros laughed once more.

"Thanks, Argyros." Tamar stood and left him sitting at the table. Argyros watched her leave then looked down at the table. Tamar had set seven gold aureus on the table to pay for her meal. His eyes widened as he looked at the stack of coins.

He had seen a few aureus in his tax collecting work, but only the very wealthy possessed these coins. To see seven in one stack spoke of extreme wealth. Tamar must have a rich supporter, Argyros mused as he took the coins into his pocket for safe keeping.

He knew they would easily support her for a year as he placed a semis instead on the table for her meal. She isn't right in the head Argos mused. Argyros will keep them for her until she is okay.

Chapter 3

TAMAR LAID IN bed as client after client, on the other side of her door, heard her tell them to go away.

She needed time to think, time to consider what to do. She was already kicking herself for leaving a year's wages on the table to pay for one meal, but she just couldn't possess that sinful money a moment longer.

Worry and fear of her bleak, desolate future gripped her heart and soul. She couldn't do this work anymore but how would she survive? That money would have helped, but eventually, it would run out as well and then what?

She thought about relocating again but she had tried that before, and it failed. Someone invariably who knew her past would spot her and warn everyone about her. Then they would push her from the community again. Those loving and kind to her would suddenly become hard and vicious towards her.

No, she was alone, and except for Argyros, she had no one. She cried hard as her fate was clear to her; there was no way out. No way to be forgiven. She was desperate for another chance, but no one from her tribe would ever offer her that. She had fallen from grace and was now an outsider.

She was so thankful that the older boy she was with that night wasn't married or she would have been stoned to death. Had her uncle and her community shown her mercy, what would her life be like now? She was so frustrated at them. These same people she wanted to be a part of did this to her, forced her out of the community and into the life of prostitution. She felt worthless when they were near. Not even one person looked at her with compassion - only contempt.

"It's not fair," she whispered in the darkness. "I made one mistake, and now I will die starving, homeless, broken and without hope."

After much sobbing and feeling absolutely desperate, she slipped from her bed to her knees and began to pray once again. She wanted a better life, a new life but how could she ever be forgiven? The teaching was clear; her uncle spoke of it often as she grew up. "If you go with a man who is not your husband, you will bring shame to this family and be asked to leave. If he is married, I will help stone you to death myself!"

She cried out to her God between sobs. Anguish and the bitterness of being pushed into a life of sin surfaced as she prayed. Never had she prayed to her God and now twice in two days. All Tamar wanted was forgiveness and a second chance to live in peace in the community and for Yahweh to forgive her.

She sat thinking. But how can he forgive me? I'm a harlot. What life could I ever have apart from who I am?

Memories of the one statement, made by the local priests, broke through her thoughts, "You are beyond hope."

"I am beyond hope," she muttered to herself as she climbed into bed, feeling drained. She knew her fate; keep working and sin against her God, or stop and still not be forgiven by Yahweh and her community, always seen as a sinner and knowing that she would die alone.

In time, Tamar slipped into a restless sleep. There were two more knocks on her door that night, but she restlessly slept through them both.

Chapter 4

TAMAR WOKE THE next morning to the sound of a commotion down in the street. She quickly put on her robe and moved the slats of her window. A large group of local people were coming up the street.

She thought maybe a Roman army commander was passing by but quickly thought better of it, realizing that he would have an elite honour guard with him, not commoners. She stared out the window with great interest when she saw the nexus of the group, the center figure. He slowly walked up the street as many circled him on the periphery. He had a core group of men near him as he moved forward.

As he approached her window, she instinctively stepped back into the shadows, still able to watch him but knowing that no one from the street could see her. A moment later he stopped and looked up into her window and directly into her eyes. His expression was neutral as he stared at her, seeing her perfectly. Tamar suddenly felt the urge to grip her robe tight around her neck as his eyes pierced her very soul. She gasped for air and took a step back in response, then fell to the floor as her knees gave out. She knelt and shook violently; her breathing labored, her eyes wide open as the memory of his gaze gripped her heart.

She didn't know what had happened, but an overwhelming sense of confusion enveloped her. She was changed somehow, and she was trying desperately to parse out what was going on. She instinctively put her nose to the floor as if praying in his direction. She couldn't help it. She had to worship him and love him and beg him for another chance.

Then it struck her; she had faith in him. She had to offer him everything she had and everything she would ever be. She was his now.

Nothing mattered to her anymore; she had to worship him and yet she didn't know why.

She quickly rose and got dressed, then ran down to the street to find him but when she entered the street, he was gone. Fear and agony gripped her as she moved to the entrance of her apartment and sat on the stoop up and out of view from the street. She stared out into space then buried her head in her lap and wept bitterly.

About thirty minutes later she heard two men talking. "What's his name?"

"I don't recall, I know he's supposed to be a prophet."

"Is he now? Is he a threat to us?"

"I don't know, that's why I invited him to my home tonight. I need to find out."

"But, Simon, you are next in importance to the chief priest in this city. Do you want this rabble in your home?"

"Haha, don't worry, my friend. I won't as much as offer him a greeting kiss. He will know his place and his status, in this city before I'm done with him."

As they moved on, Tamar rose and entered the street behind them to see who was speaking. She recognized the priest Simon and knew where the man lived.

This is my chance, she thought. I can see him there, but I need something for Him – a gift! She had little money, so she struck out to find Argyros. He had much wealth. Perhaps he would consider a loan. She had to bring this man her heart. She had to spend all the money she would ever make in prostitution in her life on one gift and give it to this man. She didn't care if she went off and died right after the encounter, she would worship him in that moment with all she had in that one gift.

***

After two hours of searching and enquiring and having people spit in her face, she finally found Argyros. She rushed up to him out of breath. "Argyros!"

He turned. "Tamar, what is wrong?"

"Argyros, I can't explain, but I need a loan! A big loan! In fact, all the money you have!"

"Are you thinking straight, Tamar?"

A peaceful grin crossed her face. "More than I have in years! Please, can you help me?"

Argyros grinned and nodded in response as he reached into his secret inner pocket and produced the seven coins and held them up to her.

"What! You kept them?" Tamar began to cry with inexpressible joy in her eyes.

"Argyros knew you were sad. Argyros knew you need food. Argyros knew you need friend, so I kept them for you and paid for your meal myself." With that, he laughed deeply then took Tamar's soft small hand and placed the coins in her palm and rolled up her fingers around them.

She pursed her lips and stared into his gentle eyes as she shook her head slowly from side to side. "Thank you."

"Ah! You would do the same for me, I am sure."

Tamar nodded. "I need to go Argyros, but can we have dinner tomorrow night. I have much to tell you."

"Argyros will wait to have dinner with you forever, my friend."

Tamar hugged her friend and then quickly walked towards the affluent area of town. She would not be welcome there, but with a year's wages to spend, it would make even her most ardent adversaries nice to her this day.

Chapter 5

IT WAS LATE afternoon when Tamar made her way to Simon's house and sat waiting in the long shadow of a tree in his courtyard. She kept her head covered and low and waited for Him to come. Gripped in her hands was the finest perfume she had ever held. Taken from the nectar of a flower, from a distant land and harvested for only a few days a year; she had spent everything she had and everything she was, for the chance to anoint Him with it. She sat and waited and rubbed the small ornate alabaster vial and wondered what He would say to her and what He could really do for her.

She was now destitute, having spent all she had and yet she knew that this day, this moment, was her last chance to set things right. She had led a sinner's life and now, anxious, fearful and desperate, she waited for Him to come and give her true hope for the first time in her life. She had faith in him, and she was desperate to express it.

She closed her eyes as she remembered the look He gave her on the street. It's as if He knew her thoughts and heart. He didn't scoff at her but simply looked at her with kind eyes. Suddenly, she heard Simon, the master of the home, arrive. He moved through the courtyard quickly. Tamar hid behind the tree. Once he was gone, Tamar waited once again.

About an hour later Tamar heard someone coming through the outer door. She subtly raised her head and looked over to see Him with four companions. As He moved towards the inner entrance to Simon's home, He stopped and turned his head to look directly into Tamar's eyes. His eyes were soft, His expression still neutral but His love was real. Tamar had not imagined it before! That's what she felt that morning! It was love, real and pure! Not the love with money attached to it or the love of a dutiful uncle. Not even the love of a mother's gentle touch but a love that touched her very soul. In that moment, His love poured into her like a high mountain waterfall into a dry pool.

He turned His attention forward once again and walked up to the main entrance and entered Simon's home. Tamar sat unable to think or move. It's as if she had been stabbed in her heart with his eyes! This man knew her! Oh, did He know her. He knew her past and her reputation. He knew her sin and yet she knew that He loved her! She began to shake as His overwhelming love saturated her very being and she collapsed to the ground sobbing.

"He really loves me, even though I'm a sinner," she uttered between sobs.

Eventually, Tamar got up, shaken and unable to walk straight. She leaned against the tree to steady herself. She looked down to find the vial and picked it up. She needed him! She had to see him. She moved to the servant's entrance and slipped into the main room where He reclined with Simon and the others around the table. He was now right in front of her!

She stood in the shadows of the lantern-lit room but knew that to approach him she would have to step into the light and be seen by Simon and the rest. But she didn't care! She had to worship him! He loved her with a love she had never experienced!

She stepped forward and approached His feet and knelt down, pulling back her head covering. Simon glanced over and instantly knew who she was and scowled at her. He then looked over to the other priests and caught their attention, then motioned with his head towards her. They all began to scowl at her. The hate poured out of their eyes and Tamar cringed slightly, then closed her eyes and began to kiss His feet.

As she touched Him with her lips, an overwhelming thankfulness enveloped her. She knew love for the first time in her life, and her tears came hard and fast. She sobbed quietly, thanking Yahweh for this man.

After a time, she opened her eyes to discover that His feet were unclean and her tears had washed them to a degree.

She immediately began to wipe them with her hair. She had spent a great amount of money on her hair to make herself attractive for her clients, and now she desperately wanted to dry her tears with this same pampered hair.

She took the perfume and broke the seal. The aroma instantly filled the room as she began to anoint His feet. She doted on Him wondering what else she could do for him. How else could she show Him how thankful she was for Him? How could she make Him understand what He meant to her? She was so desperate - so deeply desperate. She kept anointing and kissing His feet. They talked, but she didn't notice. Her task, her whole being, her whole life was for this moment. She had to show him her thankfulness and love for Him!

Then he sat up and turned his back to his host and took her hands into his. Tamar felt his love wash over her powerfully as he held her hands and stared gently into her eyes. "Look at this woman kneeling here. When I entered your home, you didn't offer me water to wash the dust from my feet, but she has washed them with her tears and wiped them with her hair. You didn't greet me with a kiss, but from the time I first came in, she has not stopped kissing my feet. You neglected the courtesy of olive oil to anoint my head, but she has anointed my feet with rare perfume."

Tamar could barely keep her eyes open, her tears flowed so hard. He continued. "I tell you her sins, and they are many." He squeezed her hands at that moment, and his eyes softened even more. "Her sins have been forgiven. She has shown me much love. But a person who is forgiven little shows only little love." He leaned in close and spoke quietly, "Your sins are forgiven."

Tamar was bewildered. In an instant, the dread, fear and anxiety were gone! She was free and felt alive! She had been given a second chance by God. She knew, at that moment, that this man was the Christ. Her heart

213

leaped as his words sunk in. She wasn't beyond hope, not now! She was alive in the Saviour as he held her hands and smiled at her; his face only inches from hers! She was so overwhelmed because the Saviour of the entire world; her Saviour was holding her hands like she was the only one who mattered at that moment. He looked into her eyes with such absolute love.

Tamar knew that no matter what happened, she was alive and had a new life in Him. She knew that it was time to walk in the freedom of this second chance Christ had given her. She began to speak to him when Jesus cut her off, gently shaking his head. "Your faith has saved you, now go in peace."

She knew Christ desired no words from her. Really, what could she say? He knew her heart, He knew her love for Him. He didn't need her to speak, and she understood that as she looked into his eyes. She leaned into him and hugged him hard, then got up and left the room without looking back.

As she left Simon's home, there was a lightness to her step to match her heart and soul. She didn't know what her new life was going to be like, but she knew that Yahweh was real, and so was the Christ.

She walked down the street towards home pondering much. She had poured all the perfume out on his feet, and yet much of it was still on her hands. She smelled the fragrance and knew that the Christ was far better than any perfume. It was time to live with hope. It was time to live in His love. She didn't care anymore what others thought of her—she was worthy. Yahweh loved her, and so did the Christ.

Tamar was finally free.

Please visit me at www.livinglifeinthegreyzone.com
The home of Grey Zone Ministries

If you have been changed or touched by my book and would like to share, please click on the Facebook tab on my website and let me know on my Facebook page.

I'm always excited to know what God is doing!

For more information about Partial Androgen Insensitivity Syndrome, please go to this website for more information: http://www.isna.org/
It's not meant to be the end of your research into this disorder, but it's a good place to start.

All unattributed quotes are my own.

Lightning Source UK Ltd.
Milton Keynes UK
UKHW012229240220
359233UK00005B/1633

Want to know what my mother was yelling at me about?
Rachael's Quest on sale September 2017

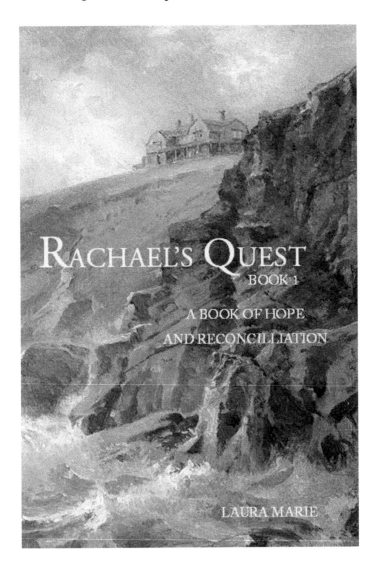